the magic of kirigami

the magic of kirigami

Happenings with Paper and Scissors

by Florence Temko
and Toshie Takahama

Japan Publications, Inc.

DEDICATED TO JAPANESE-AMERICAN FRIENDSHIP

©1978 Florence Temko and Toshie Takahama

Published by
JAPAN PUBLICATIONS, INC., Tokyo, Japan

Distributed by
JAPAN PUBLICATIONS TRADING COMPANY
200 Clearbrook Road, Elmsford, N.Y. 10523, U.S.A.
1174 Howard Street, San Francisco, Calif. 94103, U.S.A.
P.O. Box. 5030 Tokyo International, Tokyo 101-31, Japan

First printing: May 1978
ISBN *0-87040-434-2*

Printed in Japan by Oubun Printing Co., Ltd.

CONTENTS

INTRODUCTION

Books come about mostly as the brainchild of an author, but we were approached by the publisher to write a book with the title THE MAGIC OF KIRIGAMI, kirigami being the Japanese word for paper cutting (kiri = cutting, gami = paper). They wanted us to gather together some traditional and many new things to make with paper and scissors which would appeal to the general public.

In keeping with the title we aimed at a surprise quality for each project. This may not be immediately apparent when you look at a page in the book, but we guarantee that, if you try your hand at the instructions, you will experience that magical moment many times. In any case, it does seem magic that a flat piece of paper can be turned into so many different forms and decorations, only with the aid of a pair of scissors.

Everybody comes in contact with paper in one form or another every single day, whether for grocery wrapping or reading, yet we rarely convert it into playful or useful objects. Paper as an art or craft medium is often easier to work with than other media, such as paint, pencil, or clay. In the MAGIC OF KIRIGAMI we give you clear, step-by-step directions for many easy projects, suitable for lay people and artists and we hope you will be encouraged to change them, elaborate them and invent your own.

We suggest many ways in which projects can be used for

- home decorations
- holiday and party decorations
- action toys
- to entertain children
- as a challenge to the mind and hand
- to create designs for whatever interests you
- for craft patterns
- for greeting cards
- for posters
- a real magic show if you are so inclined
- and many other purposes.

The title page indicates that this book is co-authored, but it does not state that the authors live 10,000 miles (16,000 km) apart, Florence Temko in the United States and Toshie Takahama in Japan. Both are origami (paper-folding) and kirigami artists who have, separately, written several books on these subjects. In the beginning we wondered how such a long-distance collaboration would work out, but strangely enough it developed quite naturally. Toshie contributed projects drawing on the age-old traditions of Japan and Florence contributed projects with the American flavor for novelty and practicality. Then, with many air mail exchanges, we added projects, took out some and polished and polished and polished until we were both satisfied.

Through our collaboration two heritages are blended, and we hope you will have fun with the MAGIC OF KIRIGAMI.

ABOUT MEASUREMENTS

Dimensions are given in inches followed by metric measurements in parentheses. As most people find it much easier to work with round numbers, we have used them whenever possible and avoided fractions. Therefore, the centimeter measurements may not always be accurate conversions.

FLAT
PAPER
CREATIONS

It is easy to design with cut paper shapes and come up with personal greeting cards and invitations, posters and announcements. Cutouts can be lifted and repositioned until you are satisfied with the arrangement. The secret is in using paper cement as the adhesive. Apply the cement only to the cut-out and not the background. When you are ready to adhere the pieces permanently, add a further coating of paper cement.

We show a few simple shapes which anyone can cut from colored papers, such as art papers or magazine pages. Glued to folded typing paper they become unusual greeting cards and invitations with a personal touch. For a hanging poster we have connected separate paper shapes to form a clown.

BALLOON INVITATIONS

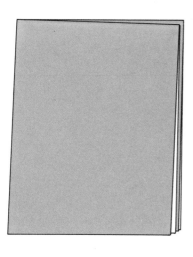

You need:
Colored paper
Typing paper
Black felt tip pen
Scissors, Paper cement.
1. Fold typing paper in quarters.
    Make first fold horizontal which will
    result in a card higher than wide.
2. Cut out a lot of balloons.
3. Arrange balloons on the folded paper.
Glue them down.
Draw in strings with black felt tip pen.

VALENTINE

You need:
Same as for balloons
1. Fold typing paper in quarters.
   Make first fold vertical, which will
   result in a card wider than high.
2. Cut out several hearts from red paper and
   glue them down. We added a butterfly cut
   from a magazine illustration.

PEAR NOTECARD

You need:
Same as for Balloons

Instead of the usual flowers, cut out fruit for a change. The pear is cut from bright pink paper and the three leaves from green. The veins and stems are drawn with black felt tip pen. And for a nice finishing touch draw on a corner of two straight lines.

SINGLE-FOLD DIVERSIONS

Symmetrical designs are created by cutting on paper which has been folded in half. We show a few possibilities for you to try and to inspire you to come up with your own versions. We have selected the designs so that a beginner can come up with good-looking results. Although some of them may look difficult at first glance, they are all made up of simple lines. At first you may want to draw the designs with pencil, but in a short while you will be able to "draw" directly with the scissors. The final cut-outs may vary considerably from person to person. After all, not all butterflies look alike.

Completed cut-outs are useful for decorating stationery, greeting cards, certificates and diplomas and for making large size posters.

MUSHROOM RECIPE BOX

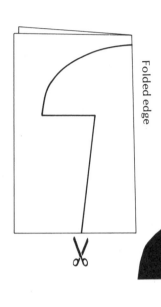

Folded edge

You need:
Paper
Pencil, Scissors

1. Fold a piece of paper in half.
   On the folded edge, draw half a
   mushroom.
   Cut on the outline, through both layers
   of paper.
2. Unfold. Glue cut-outs to a recipe box.

CHRISTMAS STATIONERY

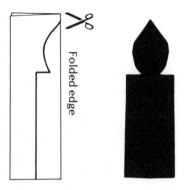

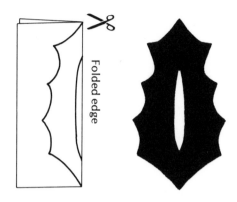

You need:

Colored paper

Blank greeting card or folded typing paper

1. Cut candle and holly leaves from folded red and green papers.
2. Glue to greeting card.

MASKS

BULLDOG MASK

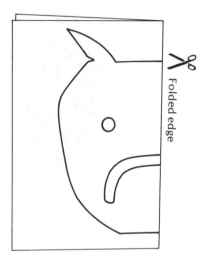

You need:

Paper

Pencil, Scissors, String

1. Draw on half a mask. For the eyes, first pierce with the point of the scissors and then enlarge the hole by cutting around.
2. Also pierce holes on both sides of the mask. Attach two pieces of string to hold the mask on your head.

BEAR MASK

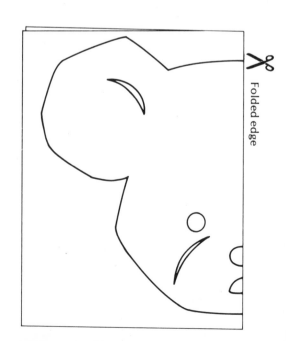

✂ Folded edge

MONSTER MASK

You need:
Paper
Pencil, Scissors, String
1. Proceed as for Bulldog.
   Cut the main lines of the mouth and
   then add the zig-zags.

CLOWN MOBILE

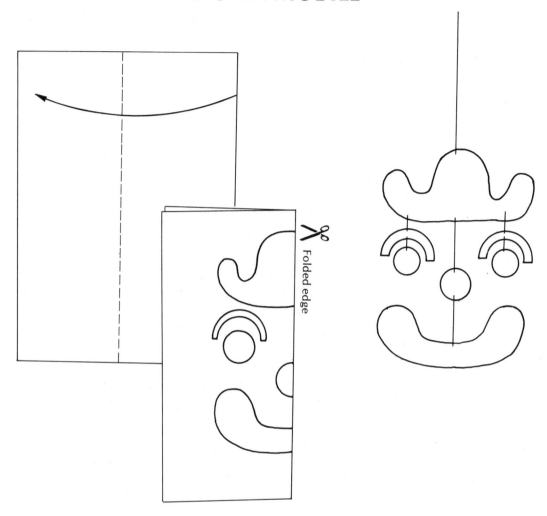

Folded edge

The clown's face is divided into separate parts which move independently of each other when suspended as shown.

You need:

Large sheet of paper or thin cardboard

Pencil, Scissors

Needle and thread

1. Fold paper in half lengthwise.
   On the folded edge, draw the clown's face in parts as shown, and cut them out.
2. Unfold the pieces of paper and string them together as shown. Note that the eyes are not connected to the mouth, as this allows more movement.

CLOWN POSTER

You need:
Same as for Clown Mobile.
The clown can be used as an effective advertisement. Add another piece of paper or cardboard and write your advertising message on both sides in large letters. Suspend it below the clown.

BUTTERFLY COLLECTION

Paper butterflies make beautiful decorations for walls, gift packages and for many other purposes. They can be made with details to imitate nature or you can use your own imagination with the help of the many patterned gift papers now available.

The instructions show how to make a basic butterfly and a few variations.

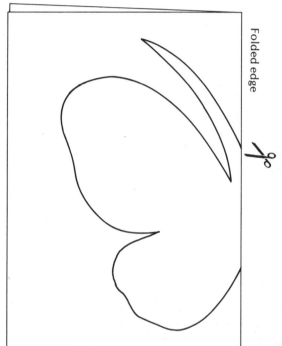

Folded edge

BASIC BUTTERFLY

You need:
Colored paper
Pencil, Scissors.
1. Fold a piece of paper in half. Draw on half a butterfly on the folded edge of the paper. Cut on the outline.
2. Unfold paper.

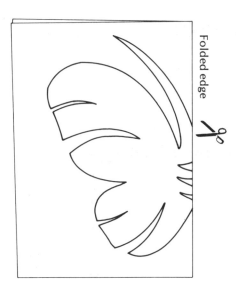

BUTTERFLY WITH SLIT CUTS

1. Make a basic butterfly.
   Cut narrow slits in from the edges.
2. Unfold paper.

TWO-LAYERED BUTTERFLY

Cut a basic butterfly
From paper in another color, cut a butterfly
with slit cuts, but smaller than the basic
butterfly.
Glue the two butterflies on top of each other.

21

BORDERED NOTEPAPER

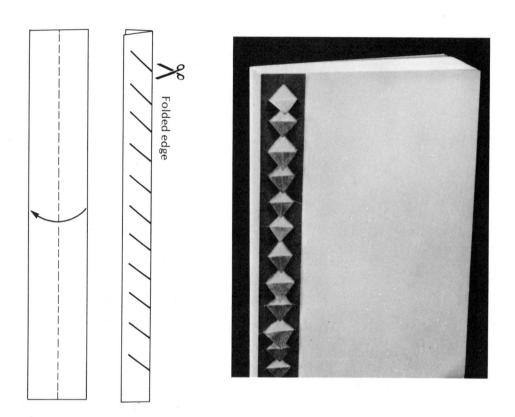

Folded edge

You need:
Notepaper
Colored paper
1. Cut a strip of colored paper 1″ (3 cm) wide
   and as long as the notepaper you wish to decorate.
   Fold strip in half lengthwise.
2. Make parallel cuts at approximately 45° angle,
   as shown.
   Unfold paper.
3. Bend up all the little triangles.
   Paste strip to the edge of the notepaper.

VACATION TRAVEL DIARY

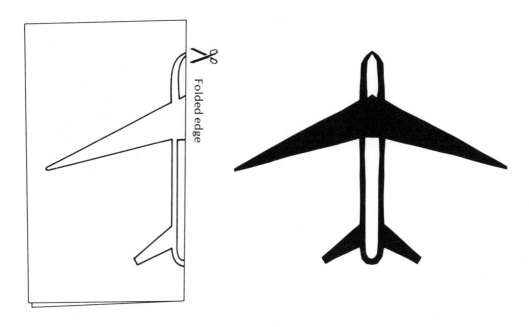

Folded edge

You can turn inexpensive blank page books from stationery and dime stores into attractive gifts by decorating them with cut-outs.

You need:

A blank page book or notebook
Plain colored textured paper or brown
    wrapping paper
Colored paper
Pencil, Scissors

1. Cover the outside of the book with the wrapping paper.
2. Cut out airplane from a folded piece of paper. Unfold.
3. Glue to the outside of the book.

OCTOPUS KITE

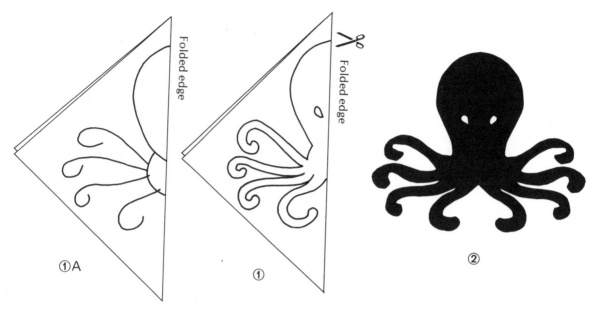

①A   ①   ②

The octopus could make a stunning design for a kite, as well as for many other objects. It offers good practise for cutting curves. Remember to hold the scissors STILL and move the paper.

You need:
Colored paper
Pencil, Scissors

1. Fold a square of paper on the diagonal. Draw on half an octopus. It may help you draw preliminary lines as shown in drawing 1A.
2. Cut out on the outline and unfold paper.

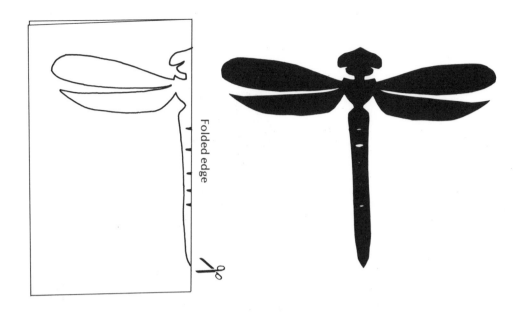

Folded edge

DRAGONFLY GARDEN DIARY

A garden diary will help you remember just when you planted, transplanted and fertilized your garden or house plants. Proceed as for the Vacation Travel Diary.

FROG

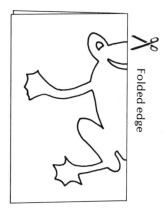

You need:
Green paper
Pencil, Scissors
Proceed as shown.

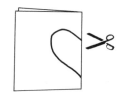

This is a more elaborate design, but always popular. In testing with lay people we found that the frog did not always look like a frog, but ofen resulted in amusing fantastics. We decorated one of them with heart cut-outs.

BANJO BIRTHDAY CARD

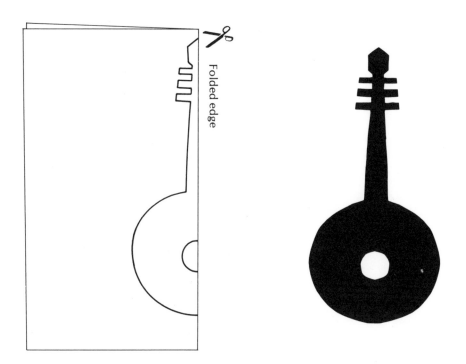

Folded edge

For the music enthusiast you can create a birthday card decorated with an appropriate instrument. We illustrate how to cut a banjo.

KANGAROO BIRTH ANNOUNCEMENT

1. Draw a line at a sharp angle to the folded edge.

2. Then add simple lines for the head, arms, baby kangaroo, legs and tail.
Cut the outline as shown by the heavy line.

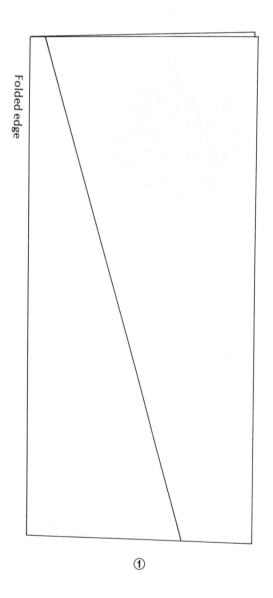

Folded edge

①

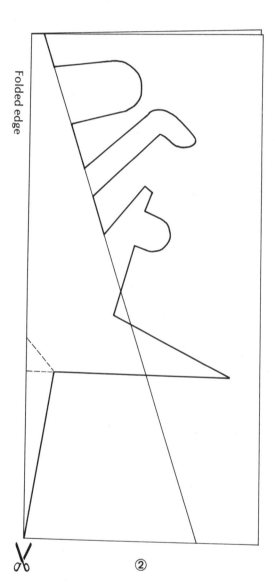

Folded edge

②

SHOWER TABLE DECORATION

Cut a large kangaroo from cardboard and place it on the gift
table at a baby shower. But why wait for that special occasion?
The kangaroo is fun at other times too.

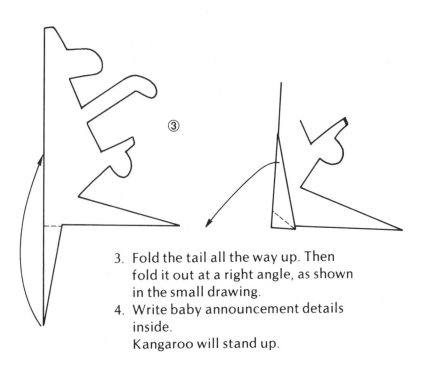

3. Fold the tail all the way up. Then
   fold it out at a right angle, as shown
   in the small drawing.
4. Write baby announcement details
   inside.
   Kangaroo will stand up.

JIFFY GARLANDS

You need:

Paper

Scissors

1. Cut long strips of paper.
   Fold them in half lengthwise.
2. Make angled, parallel cuts along the whole length
   of the strip. Cut in from one edge stopping
   about 1/4″ (1/2 cm) short of the opposite edge. Cuts should
   be about 1/2″ (1 cm) apart.
3. Now cut in from the other edge in between the cuts
   you just made, again stopping about 1/4″ (1/2 cm)
   short of the opposite edge.
4. Stretch the garland and use it to decorate for
   your next party.

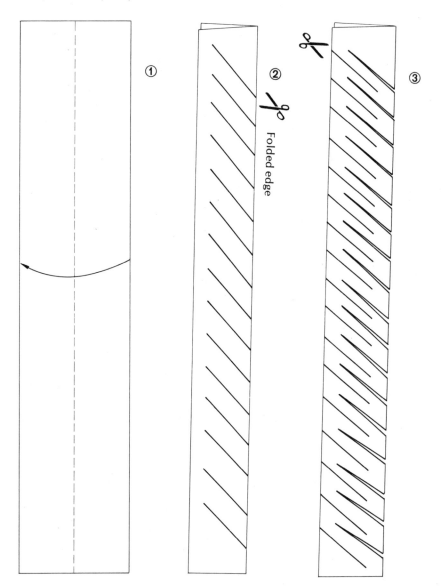

CHRISTMAS ORNAMENTS

You need:
Foil gift wrap
Scissors
1. Cut paper into strips, 6″ x 2″ (15 cm x 5 cm) or longer.
2. Cut strips just like jiffy garlands and stretch them. Hang them on the tree.

GIFT PACKAGE DECORATIONS

Use the gift wrap in which you wrapped the package or paper in a contrasting color.
You need:
Gift wrap paper
Scissors
Cellophane tape
1. Cut strips like jiffy garlands.
2. Stretch them over the top of the gift package.

MINI ROCKING HORSE

This rocking horse makes a most attractive place card and of course it goes without saying, that a child would like it as a toy. The size can be adjusted to fit a favorite doll.

You need:
Construction paper
Pencil, 6" (15 cm) Saucer,
Scissors, Glue.

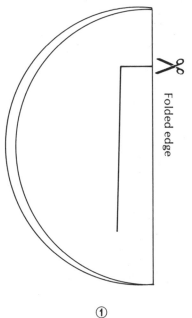

Folded edge

①

1. Cut a 6" (15 cm) circle, using the saucer to draw it.
   Fold circle in half.
   Cut a right angle as shown.

2. Swing the paper over as shown by the arrows and crease it on the dotted line.

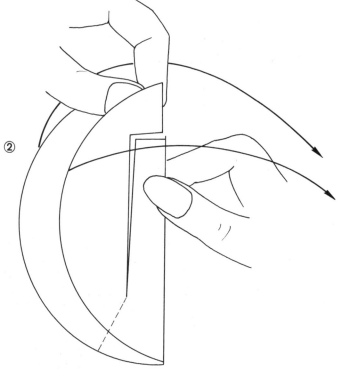

②

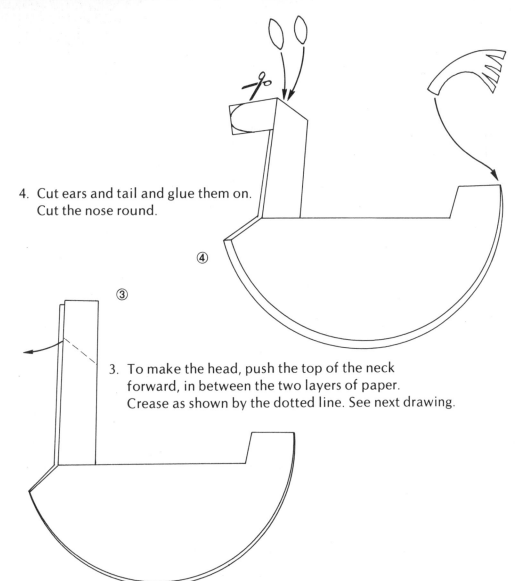

4. Cut ears and tail and glue them on.
   Cut the nose round.

④

③

3. To make the head, push the top of the neck
   forward, in between the two layers of paper.
   Crease as shown by the dotted line. See next drawing.

FIGHTING TURTLES

Turtles, when made from heavy paper, can be used as markers for board games or other games of your own invention. If you stand up two turtles and bang on the table, the turtles will move as though they are fighting.

You need:

Heavy paper

Pencil, Scissors

1. Fold paper in half.
   Draw on a semi-circle.
2. Add head, feet and tail.
   Cut on the outline.
3. Bend feet down.
   Bend head up.

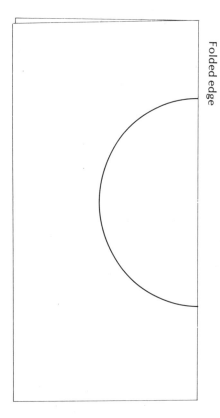

Folded edge

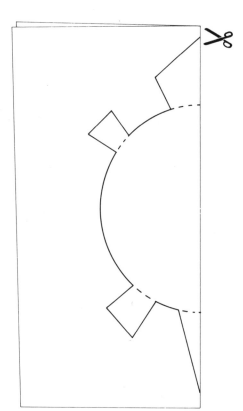

EIGHT-PANELED VARIETY

Dramatic, gratifying, versatile are the results produced when you fold a piece of paper four times before you start cutting. Every snip of the scissors is multiplied eight times, giving a complex look to even the simplest cut. We think this kind of cutting presents the most satisfying aspect of the art.

Each of the examples we show introduces a new cutting technique which can be applied not only to eight layers, but to flat paper, paper doubled over or pre-folded in other ways. Traditional and contemporary designs are equally possible and welcome surprises often occur spontaneously. Do experiment!

There are so many uses for these cut-outs that we suggest just a few as we go along. Almost any kind of paper is suitable, but construction paper should be reserved for large size objects, as fine cutting is not possible. Save used gift wrap for cut-outs which can be made from scraps as small as 2" (5 cm).

PRE-FOLD FOR ALL DESIGNS

You need:
A paper square

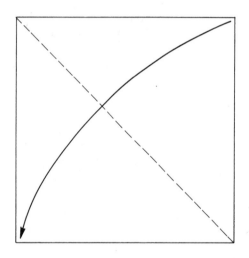

1. Fold paper on the diagonal.

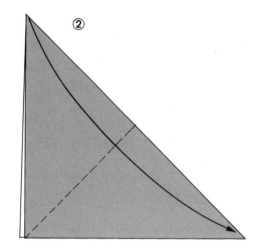

2. Fold in half.

Basic cutting principle
CUT SHAPES AWAY ON THE SIDES OF
THE PRE-FOLDED TRIANGLE.

NEVER CUT ALL THE WAY ACROSS THE
PAPER, AS IT WILL FALL APART.

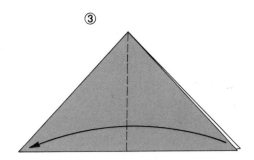

3. And in half again.

Closed corner

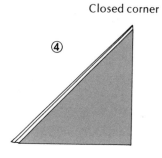

4. Completed pre-fold.

DIAMONDS

Closed corner

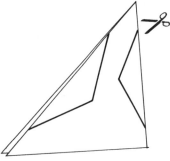

Only straight cuts here.

SCALLOPS CRAFT PATTERN

We made scalloped cuts and folded up the half circles. This strong pattern could be used as a stencil for furniture, floors and fabrics or as a pattern for a needlework pillow.

Closed corner

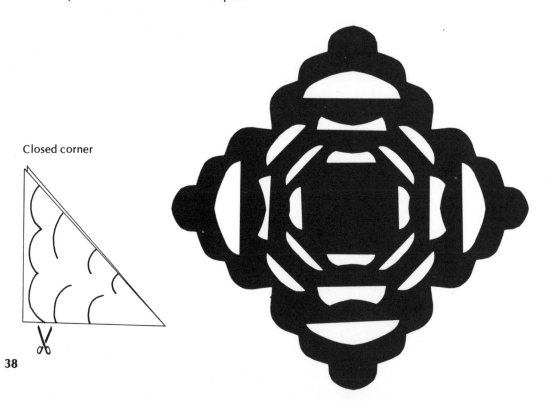

DOODLE

Do you know that you can doodle with scissors just as well as with a pencil? Random cutting produced this design. Try your own.

CONTINUOUS LINE

Draw a continuous wavy line from corner A to corner B. Then cut on the line. You do not need to follow the line slavishly.

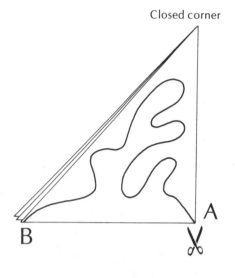

Closed corner

A

B

SNOWFLAKES HOLIDAY GREETING

This is another continuous line cut, this time made up of straight segments. Many people have trouble making snowflakes to look like crystals until they find out about this continuous-line method. Regular white typing paper or white onionskin is best for snowflakes.

Although strictly speaking snowflakes are six-sided, four and eight-sided ones are just as decorative and are easier to cut.

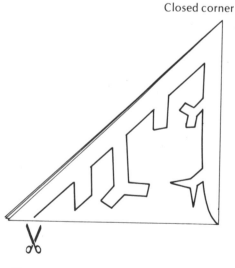

Closed corner

ROUNDS

If you want to cut a rough circle in a hurry, here is a quick method. Pre-fold paper and cut a curve as shown. Note the placement of the paper with the center (closed point) away from the curved cut.

Almost all the cuttings shown on the previous pages can be applied to rounds.

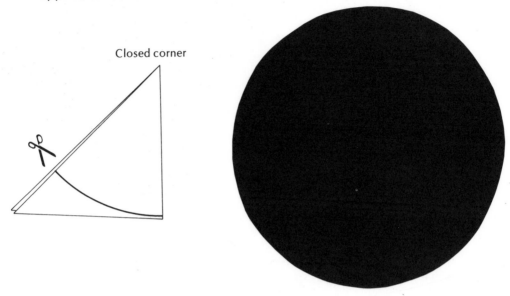

Closed corner

GEARWHEEL

Cut the paper with a curve as for the rounds. Make small straight cuts on the curved edge. Cut away alternate sections as shown by the shaded areas.

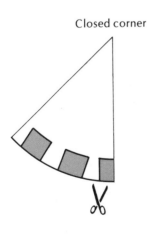

Closed corner

IN SPADES

Closed corner

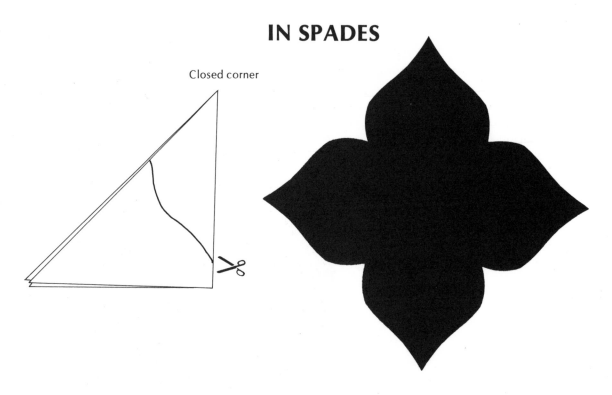

We show this cut-out in two stages. The first one is just a simple wave. The second adds some tracery.

Closed corner

THANK-YOU NOTE

The frame left over from Spades can be turned into an unusual thank-you card when pasted on a piece of construction paper in a contrasting color.

STAINED GLASS

We cut several spade patterns from black paper. When they were lined with cherry red and medium blue tissue paper they added a welcoming note in eight small windowpanes in a front hall.

HOW DID THEY DO THAT?

You may see a design on wall paper, on a fabric, on a tile or in a magazine that fascinates you. You just know it is cut on pre-folded paper, but you can't quite figure out how it was done.

Here is how: With the help of pieces of paper block out all the repeats except one and you will be left with the cut-out pattern. In the illustration the shaded areas would be blocked out.

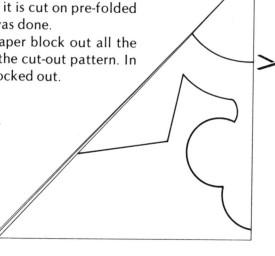

Closed corner

IN
THREE
DIMENSIONS

The sculptured decorations in this chapter are made from cut-outs which are glued or stapled to hold their shape.

STAND-UPS

You need:
Construction or other paper
Scissors, Glue, Felt Pen
1. Cut a strip of paper, 8″ x 2″ (20 cm x 5 cm).
2. Cut out an animal or any other design and glue it to the center of the strip.
3. Glue strip into a circle.

PINWHEEL

Pinwheels move when you blow on them or hold them up in the wind. Find out how to make them from squares of paper and how to use them for games and unusual decorations.

You need:
A square of colored paper, 8" x 8" (20 cm x 20 cm)
A stick
A nail with a large head
Pencil, Ruler, Scissors, Glue

1. Draw a cross on the diagonals of the paper, as shown.
   Cut part way in from the corners not all the way to the center, as shown.
2. Paper is now divided into four triangles.
   Pull the left corner of every triangle over the center of the paper and glue down the point.
3. Attach pinwheel to the top of the stick with the nail, loosely.

Note:
For wall decorations, you can make pinwheels from construction paper as large as a yard or a meter square. Display them with or without sticks.

You can also glue two pinwheels back to back and hang them.

Giant pinwheels are useful for decorating auditoriums and large gyms. Try to find some leftover wallpaper or wallpaper sample books from a local store.

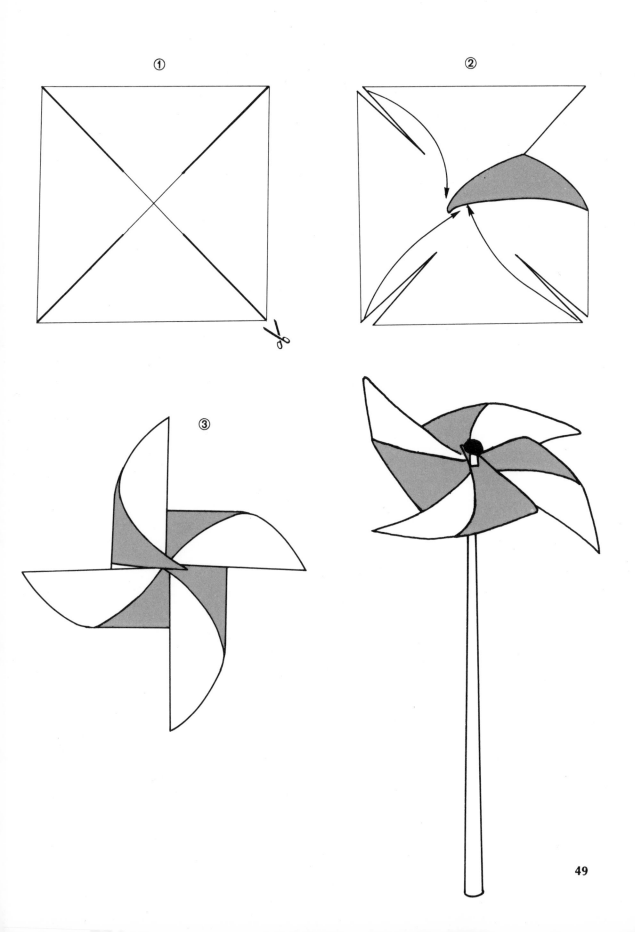

WHIRLIGIG

For this movable toy you have to make seven pinwheels and attach them to a large piece of corrugated cardboard. The finished whirligig makes a good toy or wall decoration.

You need:
7 pinwheels
A large circle of cardboard
7 straight pins
7 beads
A dowel stick
Masking or other sticky tape

1. Attach the pinwheels to the cardboard by pushing the pins first through the bead, then the pinwheel and then on to the cardboard. Don't push the pins all the way through the cardboard.
2. Attach dowel stick to the cardboard with strong sticky tape.
3. The pinwheels can be moved by hand or by blowing on them or running in the wind.

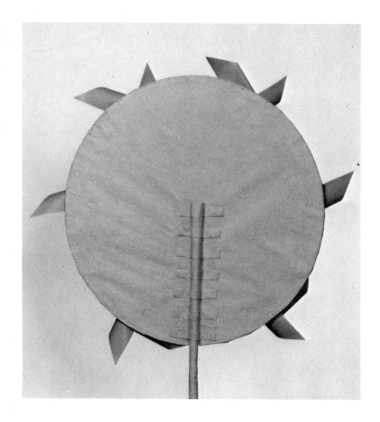

STRETCH PAPER TRICK

Here is a paper cutting trick that never fails to produce amazement when it is done in front of friends or as a magic trick. After some cutting, the paper stretches and becomes longer and longer and forms into a net.

You need:
Tissue paper or origami paper
Scissors

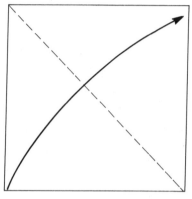

1. Fold paper on the diagonal.

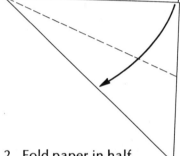

2. Fold paper in half again, as shown.

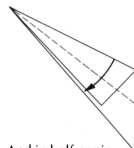

3. And in half again.

4. Cut straight across, as shown.

5. Make parallel cuts in from one edge of the paper, as shown.
DO NOT CUT ALL THE WAY ACROSS.

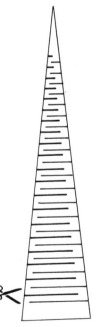

6. Make parallel cuts in from the opposite edge of the paper.

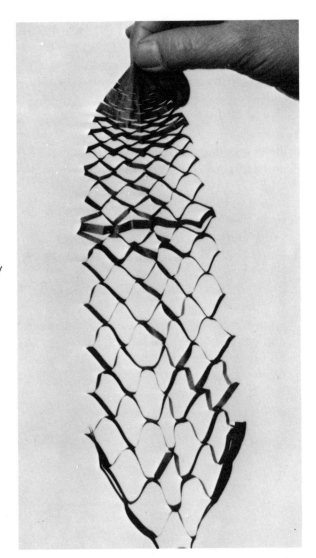

7. Unfold paper slowly
   and s-t-r-e-t-c-h.

NETTING

You can use stretch paper as a table decoration. Secure it with cellophane tape and add a few paper flowers. Attached to a wall it looks like a fish net when you add some paper fish. Be aware that tissue paper may bleed and use other kinds of paper if it comes in contact with clothing or walls.

CHRISTMAS CARD

The photographs show two views of a Christmas card which is made with stretch paper. When you pull up the top of the tree, Christmas gift packages are revealed hidden behind the paper.

You need:

A blank greeting card or construction paper
A piece of green paper for the tree, about 3″ square
(8 cm)
Gold paper for the cross
Scissors, Colored felt pens, Glue

1. Cut green paper as for stretch paper.
2. On the blank card draw the tree trunk and the Christmas gifts as shown.
   Cut a small gold paper cross and push it through the two paper slits.
   Glue stretch paper tree to the bottom of the cross and on the card where indicated.
3. To operate the card, pull cross upwards. This will stretch the tree and reveal the gifts underneath.

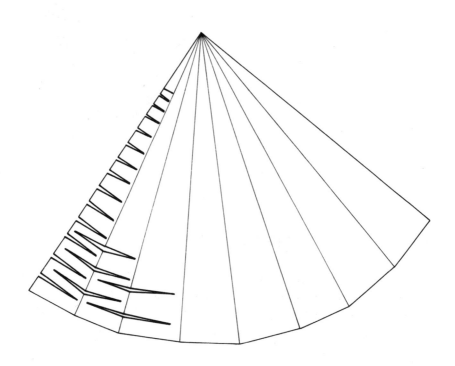

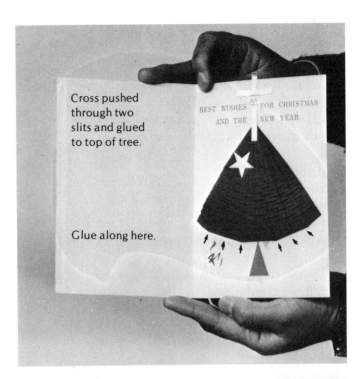

Cross pushed
through two
slits and glued
to top of tree.

Glue along here.

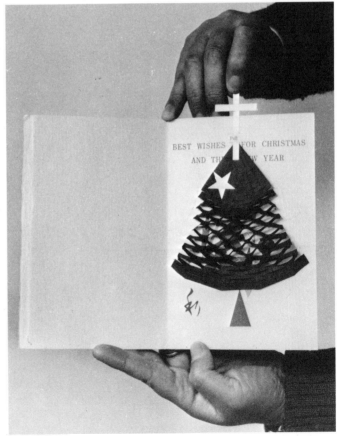

FLOWERS

The flowers can be attached to wires or dowel sticks for stems. For an unusual table decoration they can be scattered on the dining table, with or without stems.

CAUTION: The colors of some tissue papers may bleed, so do not use them on your best tablecloth.

You need:
Tissue paper
Scissors
Floral wire

1. Make an eight-paneled pre-fold, see page 36. Cut as shown.
2. Unfold paper and twist the center to form a three-dimensional flower.
3. Curl the end of a piece of floral wire and push down into the center of the flower.

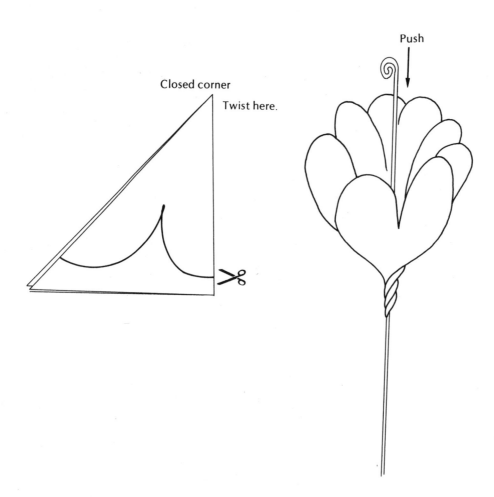

Closed corner

Twist here.

Push

CUTLERY MOBILE

You need:
Tissue paper cut into 12″
(30 cm) squares
Scissors, cellophane tape.

SPOON

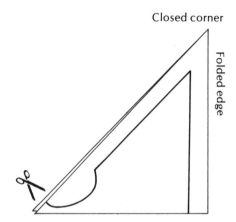

Closed corner

Folded edge

1. Pre-fold paper as shown on page 36.
   On the long edge, cut half a spoon,
   not all the way to the end.
   On the shorter, folded edge make a
   straight cut, up to the end of the spoon.
2. Unfold paper.
   Tape A and B together.
   Tape C and D together with A-B.

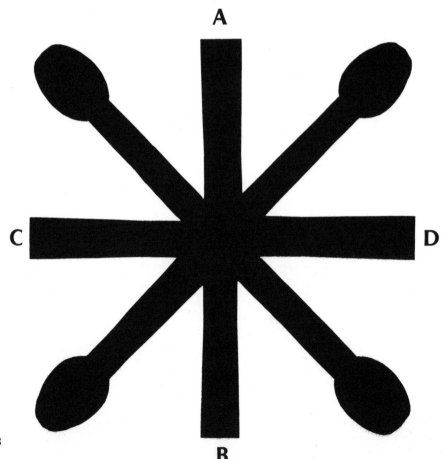

A

C   D

B

KNIFE AND FORK

In step 2, cut half a knife or fork.
On the knife, after you open the paper,
cut away one side of the blade, as shown.

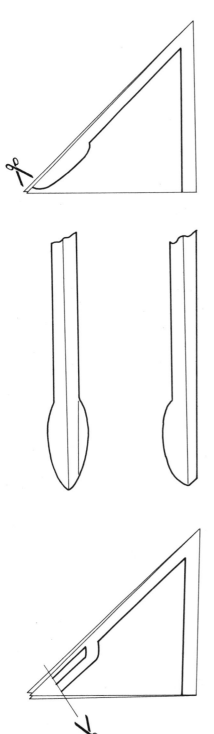

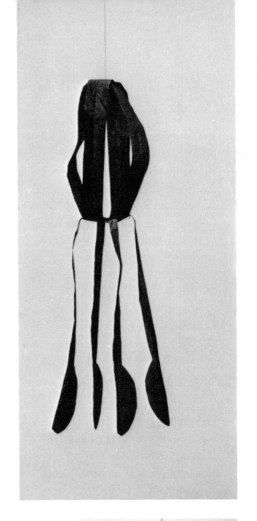

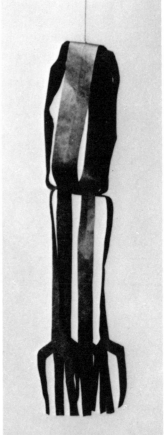

SPIKY STARS

Stars are always popular paper decorations and this pattern lends itself to many variations. A single sheet produces an attractive spiky star for a large wall decoration or a small Christmas ornament. Eight or more sheets combined make a really sensational ball, which can be used as a hanging ornament all year round or shown off year after year at holiday time. Use all different bright colors or blue and white for a most appropriate Hanukkah decoration.

We recommend it as a group activity for fund raising. One group we know spent just a few hours together and raised a sizable sum of money.

Single stars 8″ (20 cm) or larger have to be made from construction paper to hold their shape.

SINGLE STAR

You need:
A piece of colored paper
Compass or plate
Scissors, Pencil, White glue
1. Cut a circle with the help of the compass or plate.
   Divide the circle into eight sections, either by drawing or folding it in half three times without unfolding in between.
2. Cut in about two-thirds on each spoke, as shown.
   Roll each flap into a cone over the point of a pencil.
   Glue in place.

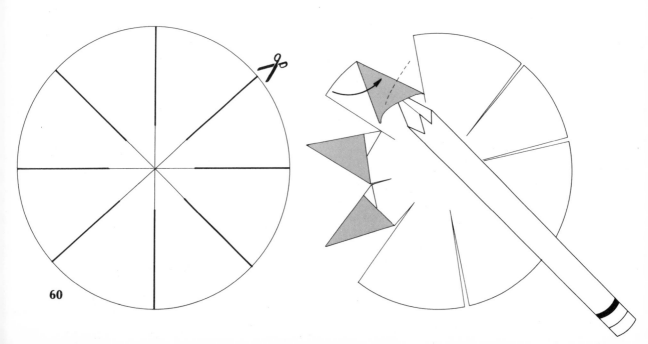

PORCUPINE STAR

You need:

8 spiky stars

2 buttons or small pieces of cardboard

Needle and thread

1. Knot a long piece of thread to a button or cardboard.

   Then pass the thread through the center of all eight stars.

2. Pull thread tight and the star will form into a ball. Hold in place by knotting on the second button.

ANGEL

Gold gift wrap paper is best for this angel, which can stand or hang. You can also attach a small paper tag with string for your Christmas card message.

You need:
Foil gift wrap
Compass or round objects
Scissors, Pencil, Glue

1. Cut two quarter circles. 4" (10 cm) diameter to produce an angel 6" (15 cm) high.
   Fold them into thirds.

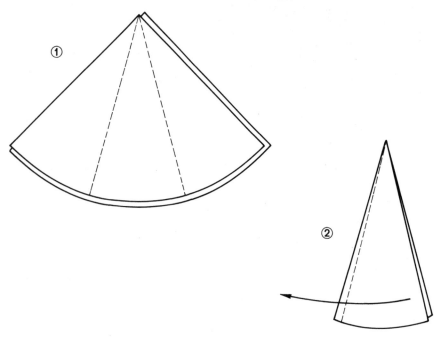

2. Fold a narrow pleat on the left by folding as shown by the dotted line.

3. Repeat the procedure on the right.

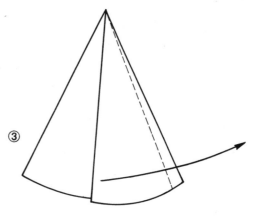

③

4. Separate the pieces and place them back to back.
Glue the edges together, leaving on opening at the top of one side.

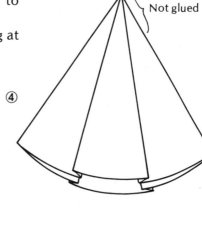

Not glued

④

Cut two

⑤

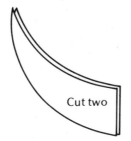

Cut two

5. For the head draw a circle 1 3/4" (4-1/2 cm) in diameter.
Add an extension for the neck.
Cut this outline on a doubled piece of paper.
Glue the heads back to back and then glue them inside the opening of the body of the angel.
Make a circlet around the head with felt pen or by cutting out small flowers.
Draw in hair line and eyes.
Cut two wings from a double piece of paper and glue them behind the pleats.

ONE-SNIP CROSSES AND FLOWERS

All kinds of decorative crosses and flowers can be cut from folded paper with just one snip of the scissors. Flowers are always popular and with different pre-folds it is possible to create them with three, four and five petals. If any reader decides to embark on a project of creating a collection of realistic paper flowers, do let us know.

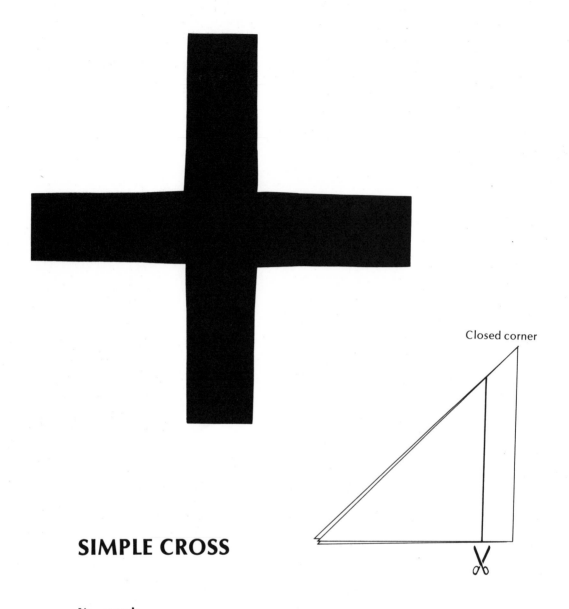

Closed corner

SIMPLE CROSS

You need:
A paper square
Scissors
1. Pre-fold square as for "Eight-Paneled
   Variety," page 36.
   Make a cut parallel to folded edge.
2. Unfold paper.

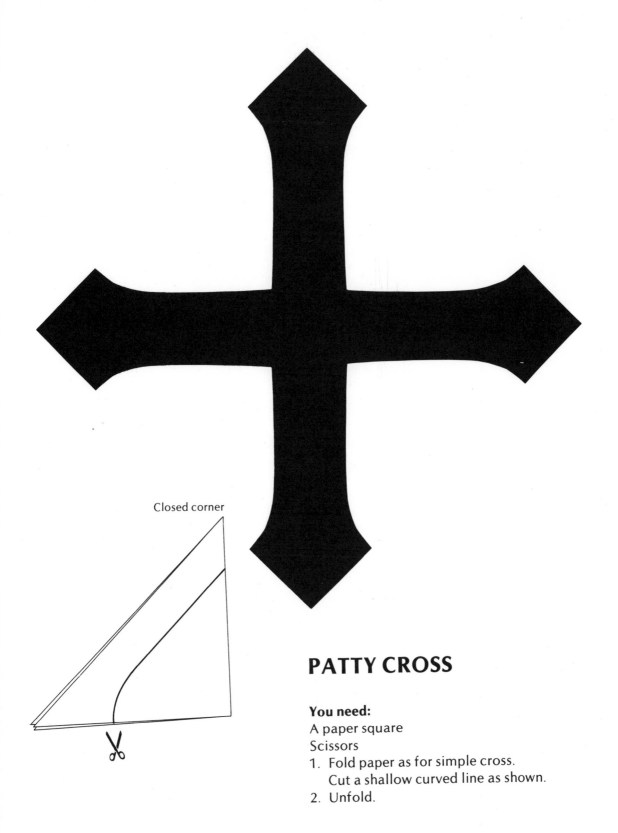

Closed corner

PATTY CROSS

You need:
A paper square
Scissors
1. Fold paper as for simple cross.
   Cut a shallow curved line as shown.
2. Unfold.

PENTAGON

Pre-fold

1. Cut a piece of paper in proportion 5 x 4, for
   example 10″ x 8″ (25 cm x 20 cm).
   Fold it in half, short edge meets short edge.

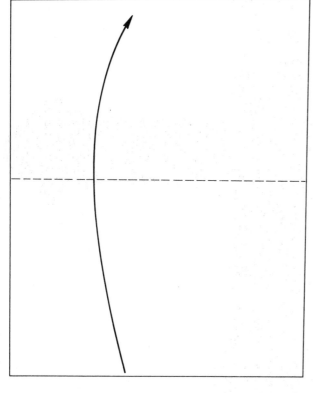

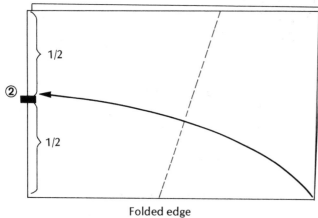

Folded edge

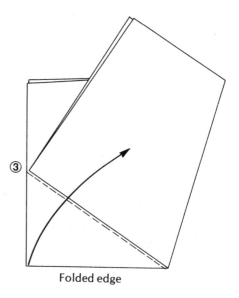

Folded edge

2. Find the center point on what is now the short
   edge.
   Bring opposite corner to the half-way mark, as
   shown by dotted line and arrow. Note corner is
   on folded edge.

3. Fold left edge over to
   the right and crease as
   shown by dotted line.

7. Unfold.

SOLID PENTAGON

6. Cut straight across the
   pre-fold as shown.

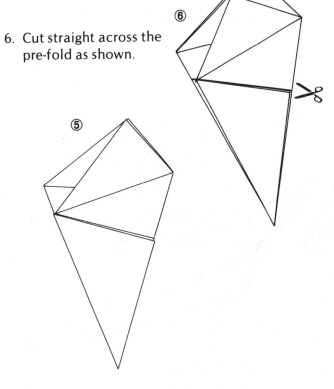

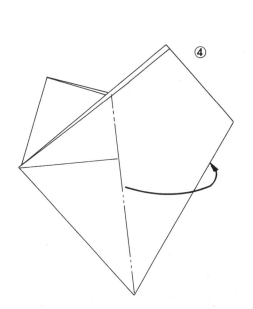

4. Fold BEHIND as shown by
   broken line and arrow.

5. **Pre-fold** is now complete.

Make a pentagon pre-fold and make a rounded cut as shown.

CHERRY BLOSSOMS

HEXAGON

Pre-fold

You need:
A square of paper
Pencil, Scissors

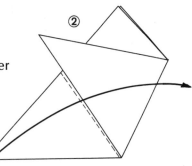

$\frac{2}{3}$ $\frac{1}{3}$

①

1. Fold square on the diagonal.
   Mark center of the folded edge.

②

2. Fold paper into equal thirds.

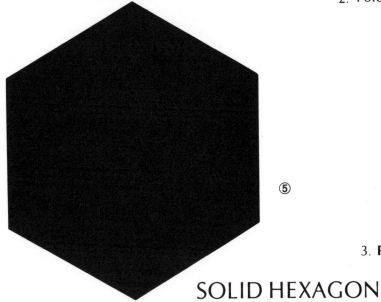

③

3. **Pre-fold** is now complete.

SOLID HEXAGON

⑤

④

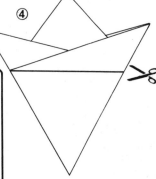

4. Cut straight across the pre-fold as shown.
5. Unfold paper.

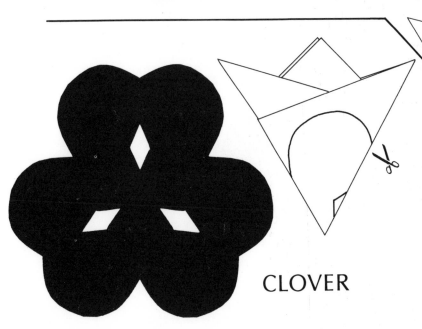

CLOVER

JAPANESE CREST

Japanese family crests, called mon-kiri, reflect symbols of Japanese life in beautiful abstract forms: plants, animals and objects. They have withstood the test of time through centuries and can be used effectively in graphic design. Many of them are based on hexagons. We show a crest with step-by-step directions and illustrate others.

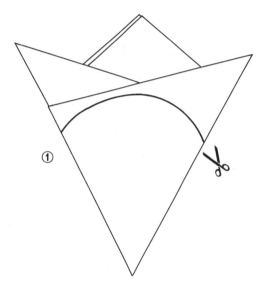

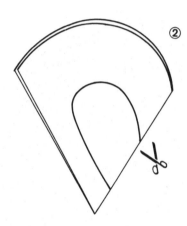

1. Make a hexagon pre-fold. Make a curved cut.

2. Make another cut as shown.

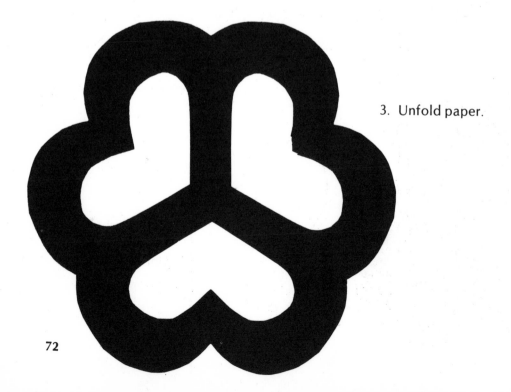

3. Unfold paper.

WILD GEESE

At first we thought these elegant wild geese would be too complicated but, by breaking the design into separate parts, it became less awesome.

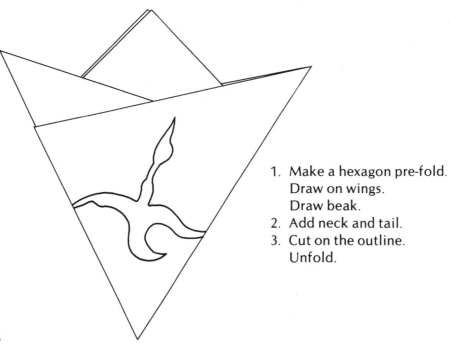

1. Make a hexagon pre-fold.
   Draw on wings.
   Draw beak.
2. Add neck and tail.
3. Cut on the outline.
   Unfold.

SIX-ARMED CROSS

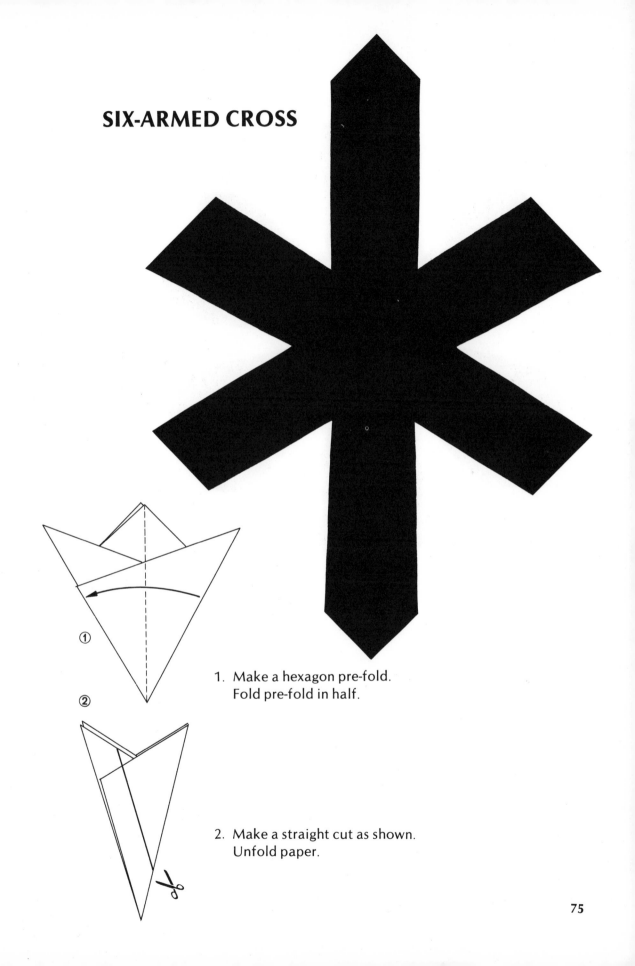

1. Make a hexagon pre-fold.
   Fold pre-fold in half.

2. Make a straight cut as shown.
   Unfold paper.

75

PRIMROSE

Fold paper as for six-armed cross, but make a rounded cut.

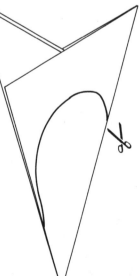

TRICKY
IDEAS

We think you will be surprised by some of the unexpected ways in which paper can be manipulated.

JUMPING JACK

This toy can be made by an adult or an older child to entertain a younger brother or sister. It is also an amusing party decoration, which can be pulled to wiggle.

The body of the jumping jack is made from a strip of paper 2-1/2'' (7 cm) wide. As this is just the width of adding machine tape, use this if available; otherwise cut newspaper or giftwrap into strips. Butt strips together with cellophane tape until you have one long strip 5' (1.5 m). The head, hands, feet and hat are made from construction paper or any other colored paper you can find.

You need:
A strip of paper 2-1/2'' x 5' (7 cm x 1.5 m)
Pieces of black and pink paper
Scissors, Cellophane tape, Felt tip pen

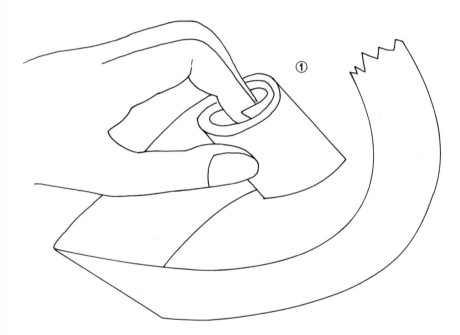

1. Wind strip into a roll around three fingers. It should finish to be about 2'' (5 cm) in diameter.

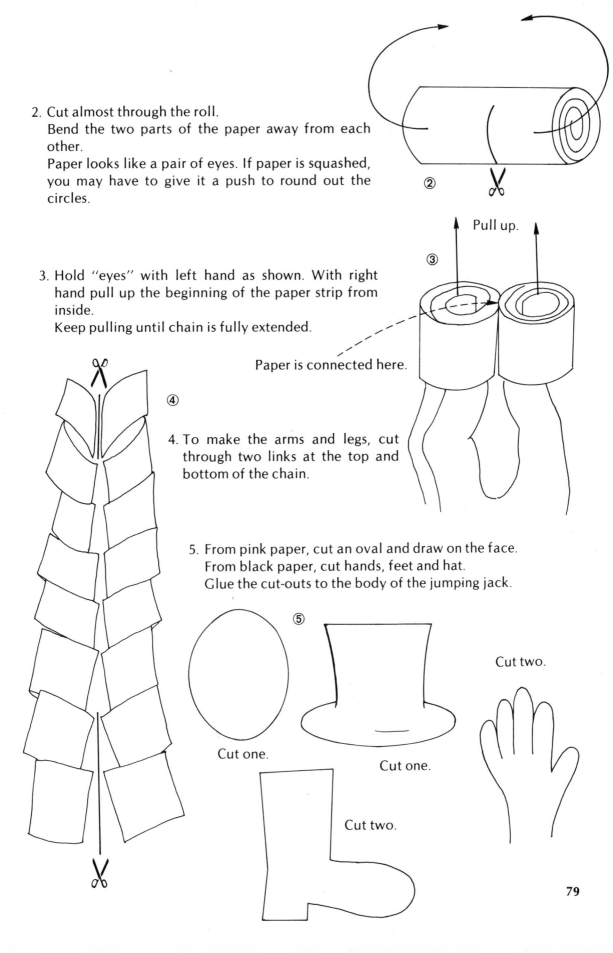

2. Cut almost through the roll.
   Bend the two parts of the paper away from each other.
   Paper looks like a pair of eyes. If paper is squashed, you may have to give it a push to round out the circles.

②

Pull up.

③

3. Hold "eyes" with left hand as shown. With right hand pull up the beginning of the paper strip from inside.
   Keep pulling until chain is fully extended.

Paper is connected here.

④

4. To make the arms and legs, cut through two links at the top and bottom of the chain.

5. From pink paper, cut an oval and draw on the face.
   From black paper, cut hands, feet and hat.
   Glue the cut-outs to the body of the jumping jack.

⑤

Cut one.

Cut one.

Cut two.

Cut two.

PARTY DECORATIONS

Attach several jumping jacks to a wall. Guests will be amused when they pull them and they jump back up.

MASKS

Make short lengths of chain, as used for the body of the jumping jack, from narrow strips of paper. Use them as curly hair on masks or as a Santa Claus beard.

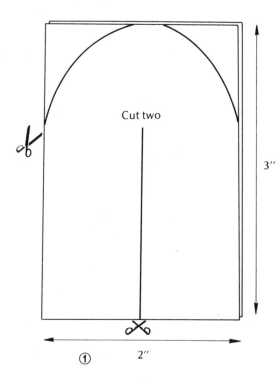

①   Cut two   3″   2″

WOVEN HEARTS

You need:

Construction Paper in red and white
Pencil, Ruler, Scissors

1. Cut a piece 2″ x 3″ (5 cm x 7.5 cm),
   one in each color.
   Round the corners at one end, as
   shown by the heavy line.
   Cut papers in the middle, 2″ (5 cm) up.
2. Place papers in position as shown
   and weave them into each other:
   Weave 1 over 3 and under 4.
   Weave 2 under 3 and over 4.

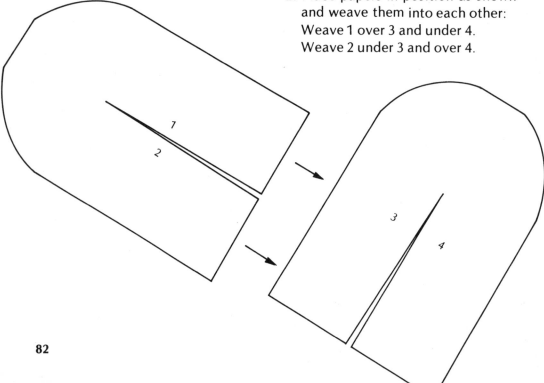

②

MORE WEAVINGS

The illustrations show the same weaving principle applied with strips cut into different thicknesses.

MAY BASKET

This is a real mystery: By interweaving two pieces of paper you end up with a basket into which you can actually put candy or other surprises.

You need:
Red and white paper
Scissors

1. From both colors cut a piece of paper 4″ x 12″ (10 cm x 30 cm).
   Fold papers in half.
2. Beginning at the folded edge, cut 1″ (2.5 cm) wide strips, ending about 1″ (2.5 cm) from the opposite end.

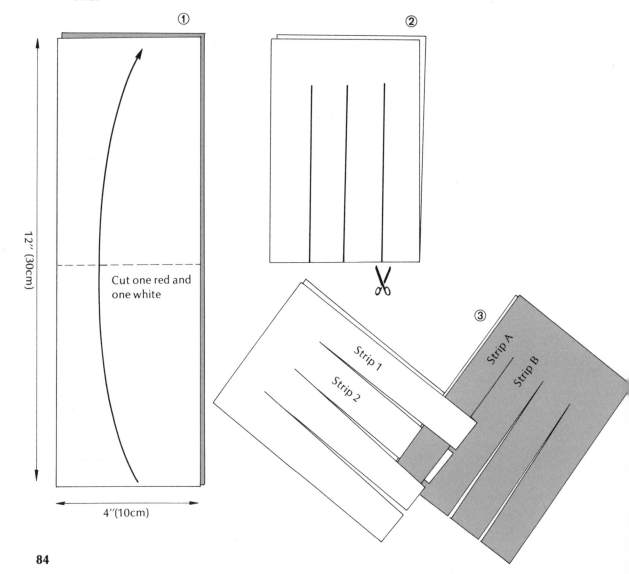

① Cut one red and one white

12″ (30cm)

4″(10cm)

②

③ Strip 1 Strip 2 Strip A Strip B

3. Place strip A between the layers of strip 1.
   Place strip 2 in between the layers of strip A.
   Continue weaving by repeating these two motions.
4. This drawing shows strip A pushed up to make room
   for weaving strip B.
   For completed weaving look at the illustration of
   the finished basket.
5. Cut two strips of paper and glue them on as a
   handle.
   We curved them for a more elegant look. You can
   also scallop or decorate the top edges of the basket.

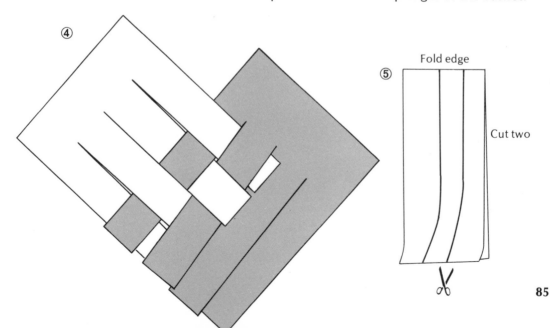

④

⑤ Fold edge

Cut two

SCUBA DIVER

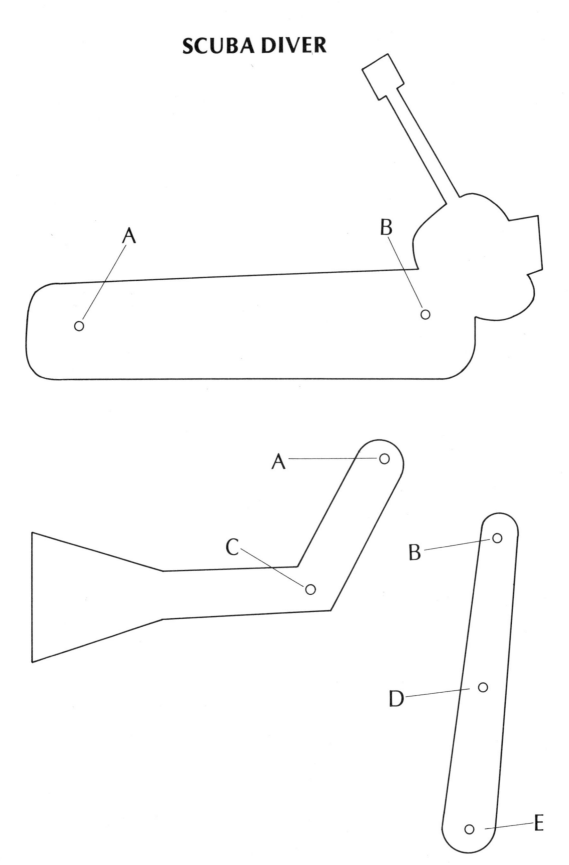

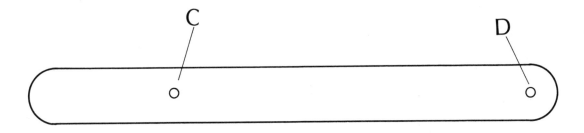

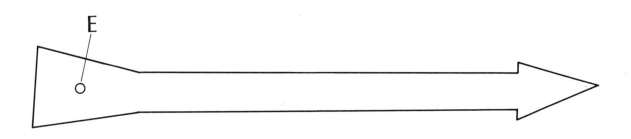

You need:
A piece of cardboard
Pencil, Scissors,
5 double-pronged paper fasteners
1. Cut the five pieces shown from the cardboard.
   Pierce holes with the point of the scissors or other sharp
   instrument, as indicated by the small circles.
2. Assemble the pieces with the paper fasteners.
3. Hold the toy on the bar below the body and move the
   spear with the other hand.

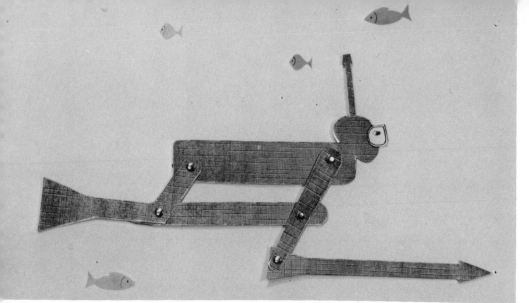

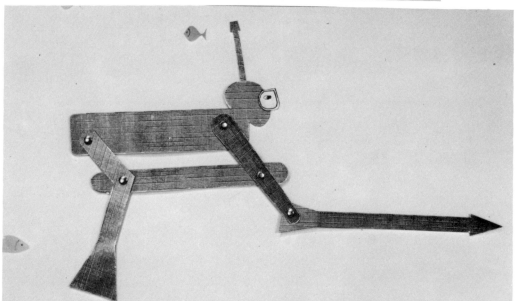

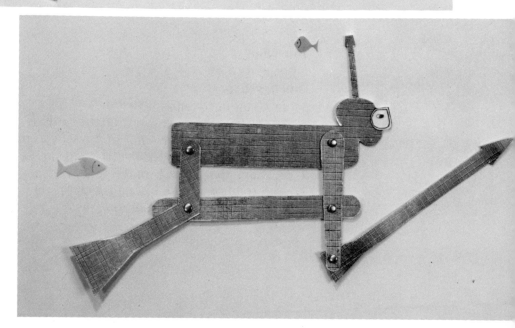

SPIRALS

Spirals are fun to cut. To make smooth curves, hold the scissors still with one hand and keep turning the paper in circles with the other hand. The instructions show how to make a spiral hang-up, snakes and a mystery moving spiral. You can use almost any kind of paper, such as notebook paper or construction paper.

SPIRAL HANG-UPS

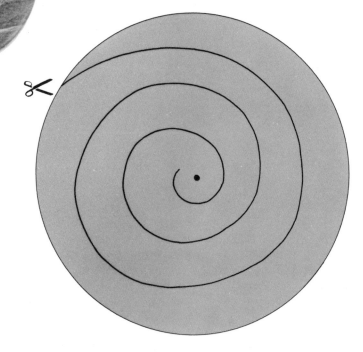

You need:

A piece of paper

Compass or a saucer

Thread and needle

1. Cut a 6″ (15 cm) circle, using the compass or a saucer to help you draw the circle.

   Cut a spiral, by cutting into the circle at a slant. Continue cutting keeping an even width of about 1″ (2.5 cm).

2. Knot thread to the center of the spiral and hang it up.

MYSTERY SPIRAL

What makes this spiral move without any apparent source of power?

You need:
A spiral made from a 4" (10 cm) piece of paper
A paper or foam cup
A new, sharp pencil

1. Cut paper cup in half.
2. Poke a hole in the center of the cup and insert pencil.
   Make a pinhole in the center of the spiral.
   Place spiral on top of pencil.

Mystery power: Place spiral near a heater and it will turn.

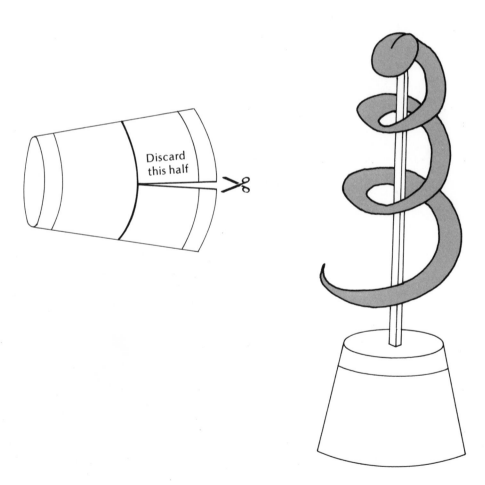

Discard
this half

SNAKY SERPENT

It is easy to turn spirals into snakes. Cut small pieces of paper in the shape of heads and glue them to spirals.

Spirals look so snaky that it is easy to make a whole reptile scene for fun or as an unusual table decoration for a birthday party. For this purpose you may be able to find some greenish or grey paper which looks snake-like.

To make snakes, cut a lot of spirals and glue on small pieces of paper cut in the shape of heads. Draw on scales.

When you are ready to place the snakes on the table, pinch them in several places so that they become three-dimensional. To create a more interesting scene, add small pebbles and bottlecaps which you can paint to look like rocks.

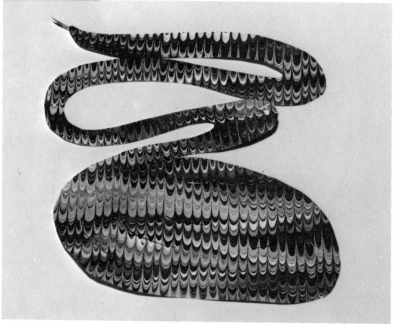

SPIRAL SCULPTURE

You need:

Heavy white paper

Scissors

1. Fold a rectangle of paper in half.
   Make the two spiral cuts as shown.
2. You now have the choice of sending the sculpture in the mail as a greeting card, or hanging it.

Note: Different weight of paper produce tight or loose spirals, so experiment by cutting more or less rings on the spirals.

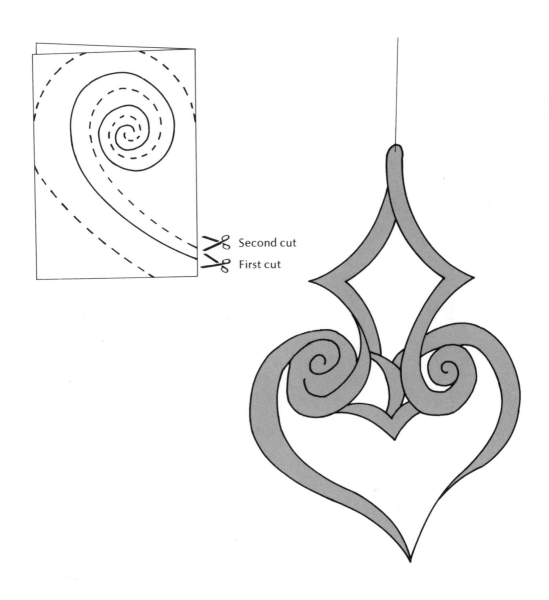

Second cut

First cut

REPEAT
PATTERNS

As you look around you, at home furnishings, wallpaper, print media and television, you are sure to find many repeat patterns. They are found in folk-crafts as well as in the most sophisticated art and are a very satisfying way of decorating.

For an amateur, paper cutting is an excellent and easy medium to devise decorative patterns, whether small enough to border stationery or large enough for a bold poster.

We begin the chapter by arranging triangles to create all sorts of effects and then apply the same principle to other forms. In your own work stick to shapes which are easy to cut: rectangles and squares, circles drawn with the help of jars and plates; hearts and fish. There is limitless variety right there, and in addition, many ideas in the eight-panel chapter are a goldmine for repeat designs.

Any shape which is repeated in a grouping, whether side by side or in a cluster or a rhythmic pattern almost always looks professional.

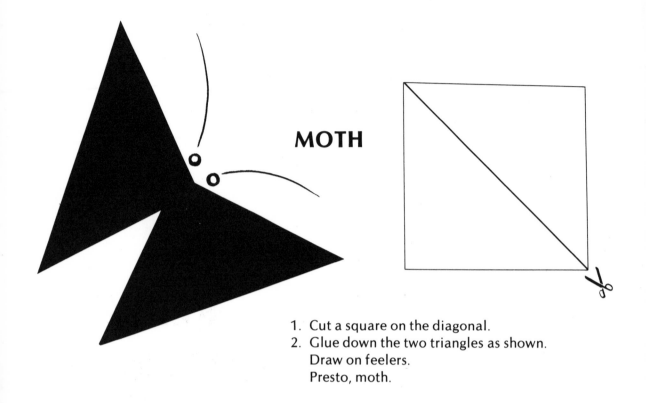

MOTH

1. Cut a square on the diagonal.
2. Glue down the two triangles as shown.
   Draw on feelers.
   Presto, moth.

WINDMILL QUILTING PATTERN

Many American quilts are made of designs composed of triangles, squares and diamonds. We illustrate the popular windmill pattern which you can multiply as it would be for a quilt; or it can be enlarged into a bold poster.

1. Cut four squares on the diagonal.
2. Glue down the triangles in a
   circular pattern.

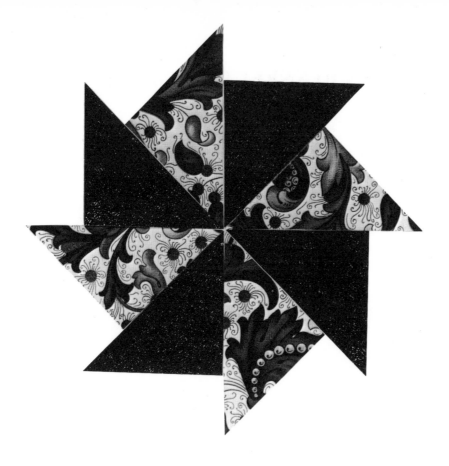

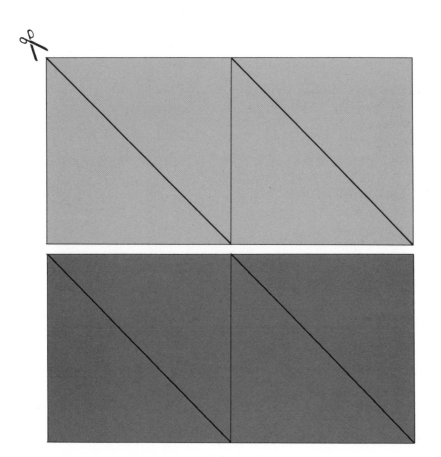

INDIAN BLANKET PLACEMATS

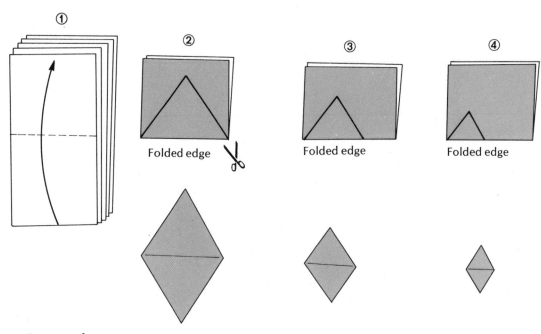

① ② ③ ④

Folded edge ✂ Folded edge Folded edge

You need:
Black, white and brown paper for the diamonds
Heavy white paper for the background
Scissors, Glue

DIAMONDS

1. Fold pieces of paper in half, and cut triangles.
   When unfolded, you will have diamonds.
2. First cut black diamonds.
3. Cut white diamonds slightly smaller.
4. Cut brown diamonds smaller still.
5. Glue black diamonds on the background. Then
   top them with white and brown diamonds.

BORDER

6. Cut four strips of paper the same length as the
   longer sides of the background paper.
7. Fold each strip in eighths.
   Cut triangles from the edges.
8. Unfold strips.
   Glue them to the edges of the background.
   On the short sides cut off any excess.

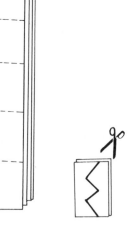

ROTATING TRIANGLES

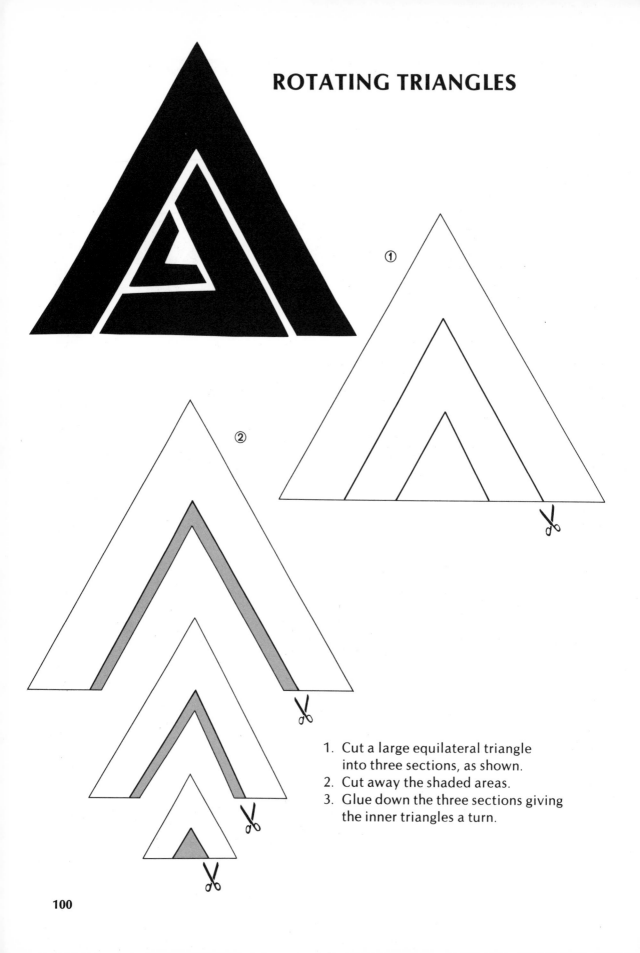

①

②

1. Cut a large equilateral triangle into three sections, as shown.
2. Cut away the shaded areas.
3. Glue down the three sections giving the inner triangles a turn.

100

BANNER

Four semi-circles are glued back to back on a contrasting background. A really simple and dramatic composition.

MANY LEAVES

Here we show how to adapt an eight-panel design.

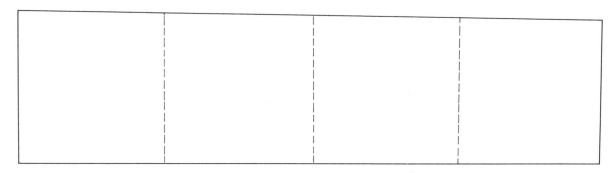

①

Closed corner

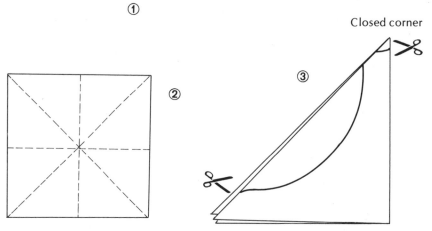

② ③

You need:
A piece of tissue paper in the proportion
   of 4 to 1
1. Fold paper in quarters.
2. Make pre-fold as shown on page 36.
3. Cut away curved section on the long edge.
   Unfold.

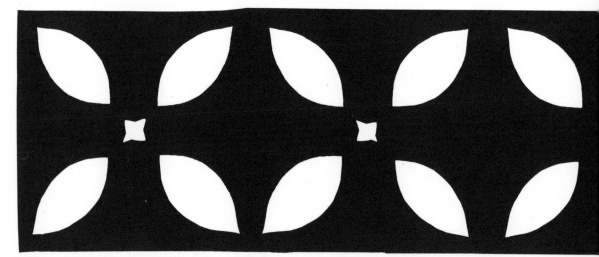

FALL DECORATIONS

The pieces which were cut away in step 3 in "Many Leaves" are glued to a piece of stationery.

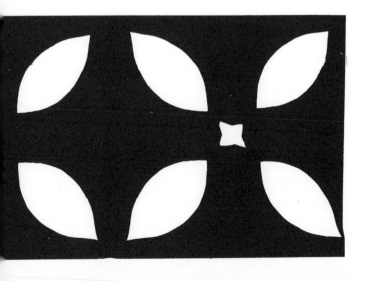

BOXES

It seems one can never have enough boxes, large or small, whether for storing small trinkets or for gifts. To remedy this situation you can make your own boxes from construction paper. Since it is easy enough to find square boxes, we decided not to bother duplicating them, but to show a star-shaped box with a lid and an open candy dish. Both are very sculptural and can be adapted to many purposes. Obviously they can be filled with candy or cookies, but are also attractive gift items in themselves. Other ideas are to hang them or display them as table-top sculptures, especially when made from heavy metallic gift wrap paper. The basic construction techniques can be applied to boxes in other shapes and sizes.

FANCY BOX

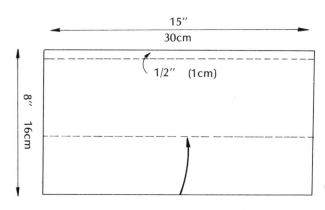

15″
30cm

8″
16cm

1/2″ (1cm)

①

You need:
Construction paper
Scissors, Glue

1. Cut paper 15″ x 8″ (30 cm x 16 cm).
   Make lengthwise folds 3-1/2″ (7 cm)
   up and 1/2″ (1 cm) down.
   The two edges will meet.

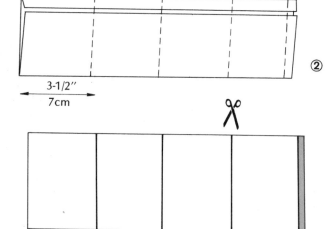

3-1/2″
7cm

②

2. Fold paper in 3-1/2″ (7 cm) sections,
   which leaves 1″ (2 cm) at the end.
   Unfold paper.

③

3. Cut on the folded lines as shown,
   leaving 3-1/2″ (7 cm) uncut.
   Cut away shaded area.

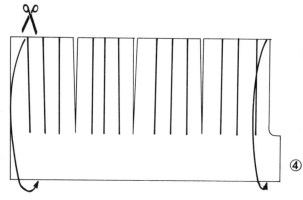

④

4. Make three cuts on each flap, divid-
   ing it into four equal sections.
   Fold the strips over the uncut area
   and glue the ends to the back.

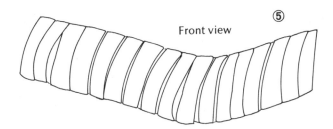

⑤

Front view

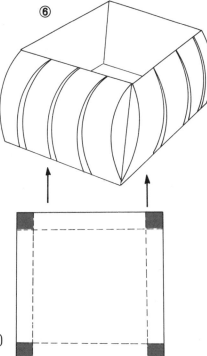

⑥

5. Shape box into a cube and glue it together with the extra 1" (2 cm).

Back view

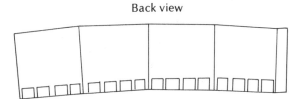

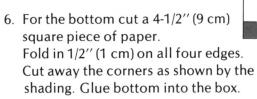

6. For the bottom cut a 4-1/2" (9 cm) square piece of paper.
Fold in 1/2" (1 cm) on all four edges.
Cut away the corners as shown by the shading. Glue bottom into the box.

STAR BOX

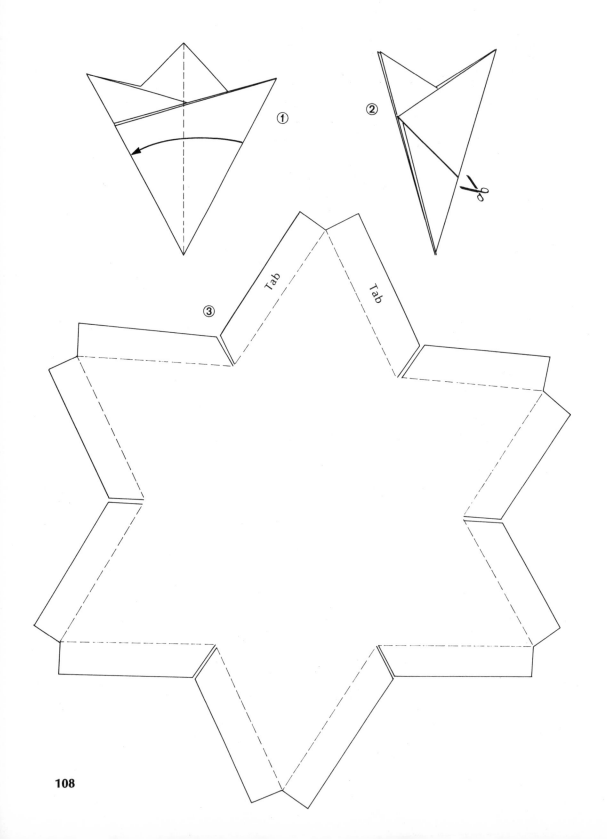

①

②

③

Tab

Tab

You need:

Construction Paper
Paper for pattern
Scissors, Pencil, Ruler, Glue

1. From a piece of paper at least 9'' (22 cm) square, cut a pattern for a six pointed star as follows:
   Make a hexagon pre-fold, page 71, and make one cut as shown. Unfold paper.
2. Place the star on construction paper and draw around it, as shown by the dotted lines.
   Add tabs all around as shown by the outline.
   Cut on the outline.
3. For the sides of the box, cut strips of construction paper 3'' (8 cm) wide and glue them together until you have a piece 40'' (1 m) long.
4. Fold up the tabs on the star to stand upright (see dotted lines on drawing). Glue the paper strip against the tabs, all around the star, making crease to conform to the points.
5. For the lid of the box cut another star exactly the same as directed in step 2.
   In step 3 cut strips of construction paper 1'' (3 cm) wide and attach them to the star as for the bottom part of the box in step 4.

JEWISH HOLIDAY BOX

Decorate the star box with Jewish symbols. We show it with the shofar horn.

The star box can be made in different sizes as a table decoration or a mobile.

PAPER DOLLS

Everybody knows what paper dolls look like, but not everybody knows how to cut them. Basically a strip of paper is folded into pleats and half the shape of a person is cut on the pleats. The trick, of which many people are not aware, is that the figure must reach across to the opposite edge, otherwise the chain falls apart.

Once the principle is understood, any kind of design can be substituted for dolls. We show you paper dolls in a row; boys *and* girls holding hands around a birthday cake; and a Christmas tree series.

TRADITONAL PAPER DOLLS

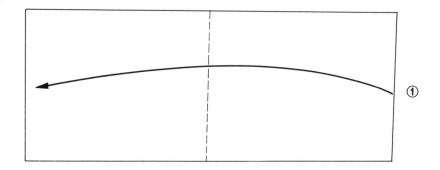

①

②

③

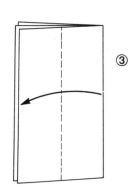

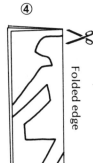

④

Folded edge

You need:

A strip of paper about 10″ x 4″ (25 cm x 10 cm)
Half a piece of typing paper is good
Pencil, Scissors

1. Fold paper in half.
2. Fold in half again.
3. And fold in half once more.
4. Place paper exactly as shown with cut edges of paper to the left.

   Draw in half a person on the folded edge on the right. The arm is the connecting link and must reach the opposite edge.

   Cut out on the line through all layers of the paper.

MERRY CHRISTMAS TREES

A forest of trees cut from green construction paper is glued on a red background for a cheery Christmas card.

First we folded a standard piece of red construction paper size 12″ x 9″ (30 cm x 21 cm), into quarters. Then we folded a green strip of paper 12″ x 3″ (30 cm x 7.5 cm) four times, in the same way as for the paper dolls. When cut, this produced four trees. We pasted one of them on the front of the card and folded the other three to the inside.

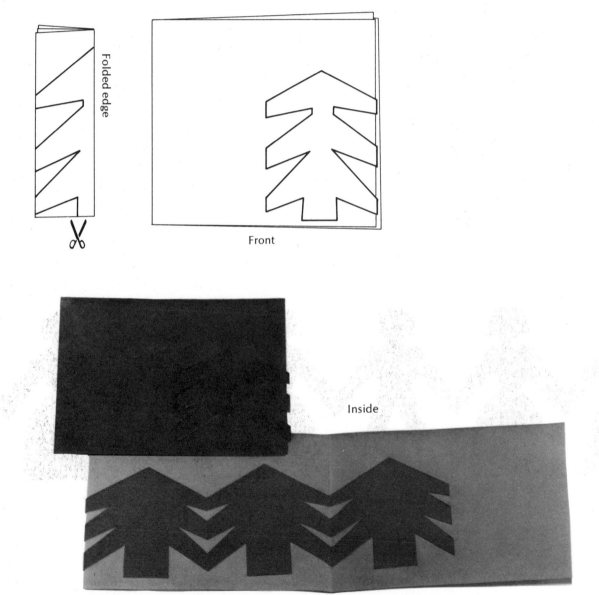

Folded edge

Front

Inside

BIRTHDAY CAKE

This birthday cake is decorated with a row of girls and boys holding hands. They are cut from one pleated strip.

Cut the half-figure of a boy on one edge and the half-figure of a girl on the other edge with their hands meeting in the middle. Your finished cut-out will have half-figures at both ends. Cut them off or glue them together into another complete person.

To circle all around the cake either use a long strip of paper to fit or glue several shorter strips together.

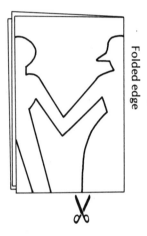

Folded edge

CUT-APARTS

Take a dark piece of paper and cut it into sections. Glue them on a white piece of paper, leaving spaces in between. The strong contrast created by the repetition of the same forms in black and white almost always assures a well balanced design.

We recommend that you use rubber cement for gluing, as it permits re-arranging of the forms without injuring the background.

STRAIGHT LINES

You need:
Black paper
White paper
Scissors
Rubber cement

1. Cut a 3'' (8 cm) square of black paper into uneven strips.

2. Paste the strips on the white paper.

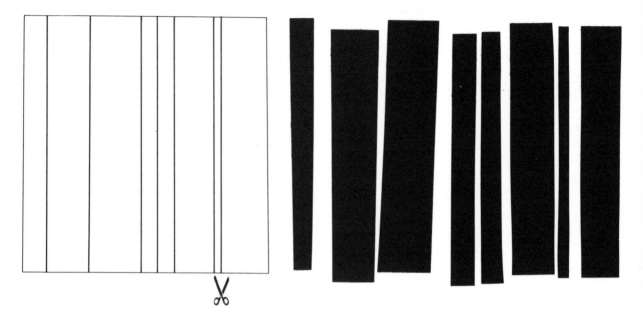

VARIATION

Here the paper is cut into straight and curved lines to show just one of many variations which are possible. You can also mix up two colors.

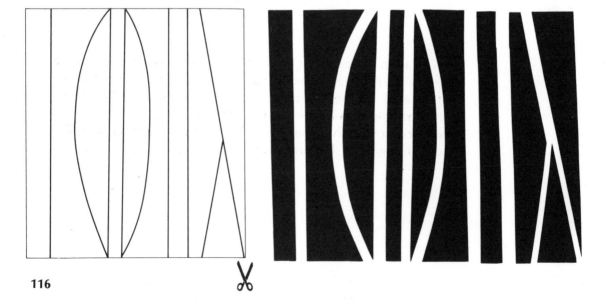

TREE

We cut apart a circle and found it looked like a tree top, which only needed a trunk to complete it.

SWIMMING FISH

You need:
Thin cardboard
Tissue paper
Pencil, Scissors
Dowel stick
Needle and thread

1. Draw shape of a fish on the cardboard. Cut fish into five parts as shown.
2. Glue two or three narrow strips of tissue paper to the back of the fish, leaving a little space between the parts.
3. String the parts to hang from the dowel stick as shown.

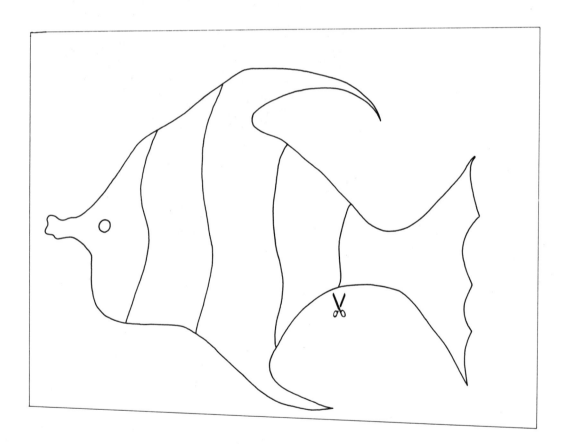

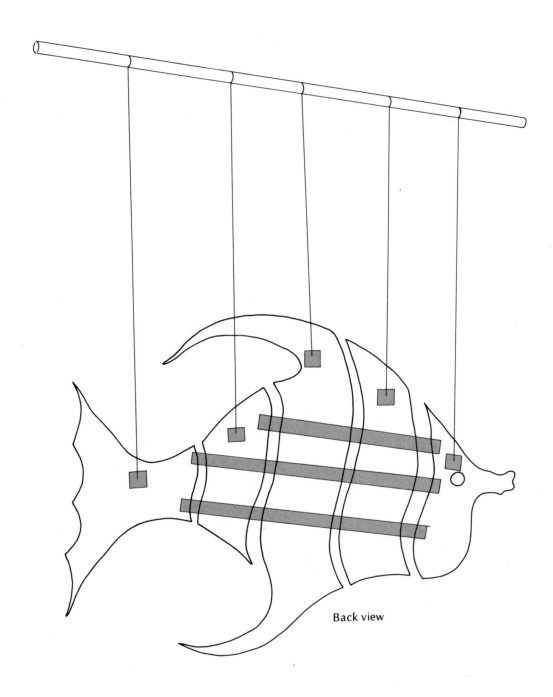

Back view

WALL MASK

Here we cut an oval in half, placed the two halves on top of each other and cut the features in from the straight edges.

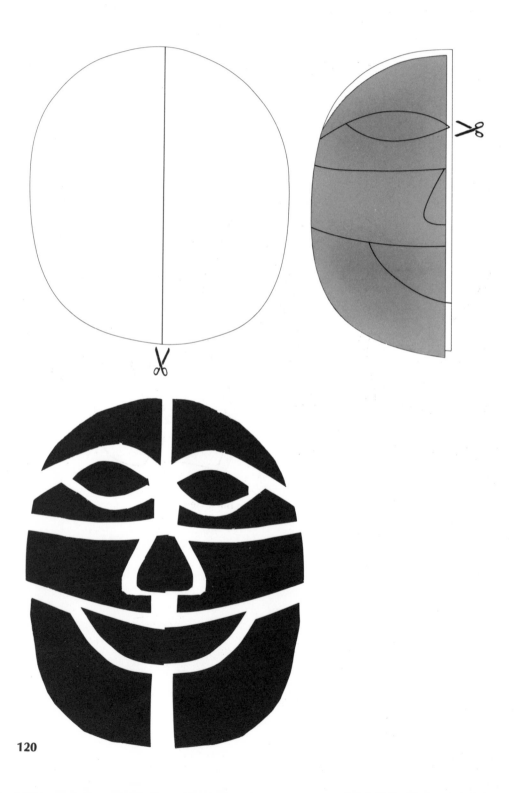

FLIPPED CUT-APARTS

We show two examples of flipped cut-aparts. The first one is done with straight cutting to show a simple, but effective design. In the second cut-apart employs the same principle by repeating a curve in different sizes.

You need:

Construction paper or any other paper
   colored the same on both sides
Scissors
Rubber cement or glue

1. Cut a shape beginning and ending
   the cut on the same edge.
2. Flip over the cut shape and glue
   it next to the original paper.

CALENDAR

Cut-aparts are well suited for making calendars, as the bold positive-negative shapes unify any twelve designs which may otherwise be unrelated.

We show the tree mounted on heavy white paper for the month of September and the name of the month of June spelled out. All the letters are cut from the same size rectangle. Each individual letter is cut in very broad block form and then sliced in half. Names of other months can be displayed in the same manner in full or abbreviated form. Some ideas for other months are Easter eggs, beach waves and Christmas candles.

MARCH

SUN	MON	TUES	WED	THURS	FRI	SAT
			1	2	3	4
5	6	7	8	9	10	11
12	13	14	15	16	17	18
19	20	21	22	23	24	25
26	27	28	29	30	31	

JUNE

SUN	MON	TUES	WED	THURS	FRI	SAT
				1	2	3
4	5	6	7	8	9	10
11	12	13	14	15	16	17
18	19	20	21	22	23	24
25	26	27	28	29	30	

SEPTEMBER

SUN	MON	TUES	WED	THURS	FRI	SAT
					1	2
3	4	5	6	7	8	9
10	11	12	13	14	15	16
17	18	19	20	21	22	23
24	25	26	27	28	29	30

PAPER APPLIQUE

Paper applique is a way of painting pictures by gluing shapes on a background. As we have stressed throughout the book, paper shapes can be moved about easily with the help of paper cement, until a satisfactory effect is achieved. In paper applique you can combine all the paper cutting techniques you know. Create your own designs or reproduce famous paintings, magazine illustrations, postcards and advertisements.

The finished pictures are obviously suitable for framing, but don't stop there. Use them for banners, posters, and patterns for decoupage, needlework, woodcraft and other hobbies. When you have come up with a particularly good design you may wish to repeat it as a gift or for sale or fund-raising.

BULL'S EYE

The boldness of a bull's eye is a sure attention getter. Repeat the design in a large size for a poster.

You need:

Paper in at least two colors
Compass, or plates and jar lids
Scissors, Pencil, Glue

1. With the aid of compass or other round objects, draw circles in different sizes. Cut them out.
2. Glue them on top of each other.

CHRISTMAS ORNAMENTS

Paste small bull's eyes on both sides of plastic jar lids. Pierce a hole for hanging.

RAINBOWS

Cut a completed bull's eye in quarters. Glue the pieces on corners of report and book covers or on gift packages.

Green paper

HUMMINGBIRD

Our hummingbird is bright green, with hot pink applique on the body and the tail feathers. You can, of course, choose your own colors.

You need:

Green and hot pink art paper
Tracing paper
Carbon paper
Yellow cardboard or posterboard
Pencil, Scissors, Glue

1. Place tracing paper over the hummingbird and trace the outline as well as the smaller body and the circles on the tail feathers.
2. Now shift tracing and carbon papers on to the green art paper.
   Draw around the outline. Remove tracing and carbon papers and cut out the bird.
3. Place tracing and carbon papers on hot pink paper. Trace around the smaller body and the circles on the tail feathers.
4. Glue green bird to yellow cardboard. Glue pink cut-outs on the green bird. Draw in eye.

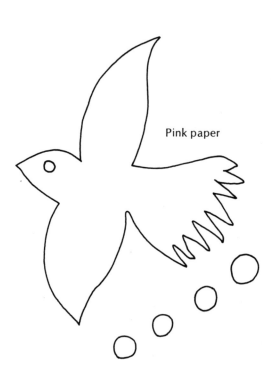

Pink paper

129

BLOOMING GARDEN

On the watering can we demonstrate how to make cuts in the middle of the paper, called inside cutting. Up to now we have done most cutting in from the edges, but how do you get inside? You need a small pair of pointed scissors, with which to pierce a hole. This gives you room to insert the blade of the scissors to cut away as much as you want.

The flowers are made with the fold-and-cut method shown in previous chapters.

This garden can be made as a large mural for the kitchen or porch or the wall of a child's room.

TORN PAPER PICTURES

In Japan pictures made with torn paper shapes are an established craft called *chigiri-e*. We illustrate this with birds in flight.

Long fibered Japanese papers tear beautifully into soft edges, but other kinds of paper can be torn or cut to achieve a similar effect.

FILL-IN-THE BLANKS CHART

This chart shows how different procedures can be combined. We believe it will help anyone come up with unusual ideas and will be invaluable to anyone interested in mastering the art of papercutting.

In papercutting two main elements are involved:
1. *Paper Preparation*
   Paper can be used flat or folded before cutting
2. *Cutting Procedures*
   Cutting methods can be broken down into six main categories.

These two concepts form the basis of this systematic chart:

Paper preparations are listed in vertical columns.

Cutting Procedures are listed in horizontal columns.

By cross charting we have filled in the squares with projects shown in the book, leaving empty spaces for you to fill with the names of your own designs.

Beyond that, you can use more than one cutting procedure in one graphic or construction. The possibilities are limitless, and we leave you to dream up your own artistic creations.

FILL-IN-THE-BLANKS CHART

PAPER PREPARATION	CUTTING PROCEDURES					
	Parallel Cuts	Geometric Cuts	Edge Cuts	Silhouette	Interior Cutting	Spiral
Flat	Rotating Triangles, p.100 Straight Lines, p.116	Moth, p.96	Tree, p.117	Balloon Invitations, p.10 Valentine, p.10 Pear notecard, p.10	Blooming Garden, p.130	Spiral Hang-up p.90
Folded Once	Bordered Notepaper, p.22 Jiffy Garlands, p.30		Butterfly, p.20 Banjo, p.27	Mushroom, p.14 Christmas Stationery, p.15 Bulldog, p.16 Frog, p.26		Spiral Sculpture, p.94
Pleated		Merry Christmas Trees, p.113		Paper Dolls, p.112		
Four-layered*						
Eight-layered	Stretch Paper p.52	Diamonds, p.38 Scallops Craft Pattern p.38	In Spades, p.42 Gearwheel, p.41	Cutlery Mobile, p.58	In Spades, p.42	
Other Pre-fold	Japanese Crest, p.72	Many Leaves, p.102		Wild Geese, p.74		

*Note: For lack of space we have not shown any four-layered cuts. They are produced on paper folded in half and in half again.

ABOUT PAPERS

Basically any kind of paper is suitable for the projects in *THE MAGIC OF KIRIGAMI*. In some instances we have made specific suggestions. The following paper are the most popular for general work and easily available.

NEWSPRINT: Least expensive. Black or colored inks create interesting patterns. Obtainable unprinted in pads in dime stores and stationery departments of other stores. Fine for experimenting and projects designed for a short life. Paper yellows after a few weeks or months.

TYPING PAPER: Generally available in white and pastel colors. Large stationery stores and print shops may also carry strong colors, such as bright greens and hot pinks. Typing paper is excellent for school projects and occasions where large numbers of inexpensive decorations are required. Typing paper comes in many qualities, including watermarked bond. It is easy to cut large numbers into a specific size, especially if you need squares.

GIFT WRAP PAPER: Sold in different weights. Heavier weights are better for larger size projects. Gift wrap offers the most exciting variety of patterns and colors.

KRAFT PAPER: Don't overlook ordinary brown wrapping paper, whether collected from discarded shopping bags and wrappings or bought in a stationery store. Most kraft papers are treated to withstand heavy use.

CONSTRUCTION PAPER: The old standy for almost all kinds of paper work. Quality has been improved over the years, yielding smoother textures, brighter colors and fade resistance. Look for two-tone construction paper, with different colors on the front and the back of the sheet.

TISSUE PAPER: Fantastic assortment of colors. Surprisingly strong. Overlap colors for unusual effects.

WATER COLOR PAPER: White. Very strong. Made from 100% rag and can be wetted and shaped.

ART PAPER: A somewhat general term applied to colored paper.

OAK TAG: Thin cardboard. Comes in many colors. Suitable for posters and three-dimensional displays.

VELOUR PAPER: Its velvety textured surface gives a rich appearance to many projects. Try it for animals.

GUMMED PAPER: Obtainable in stationery and art stores.

SELF-STICK PLASTIC SHEETING: Wonderful for decorative projects. It is sold in rolls in hardware stores and departments by brand names such as Con-Tact® or Fabulon.

ORIGAMI PAPER: Popular Japanese paper in clear bright colors, cut into squares 6-1/2'' (16 cm) and larger. Art supply stores as well as some gift and stationery stores carry it.

WASHI PAPER: Heavier weight, hand-made Japanese paper often with small repetitive designs. Also sold in packs like origami paper, or in full size sheets.

PAPER SUPPLIERS

Arthur Brown & Bro., Inc.,
2 West 46th Street,
New York, N.Y. 10036. U.S.A.

Largest art supply distributor. Will send catalog.

Andrews/Nelson/Whitehead,
31-10 48th Avenue,
Long Island City, N.Y., 11101, U.S.A.

Specialists for fine papers from all over the world.

Flax's
250 Sutter Street,
San Francisco, California, 94108, U.S.A.

Art suppliers.

Paperchase Products Ltd.,
216 Tottenham Court Road,
London, W.L. England.

Immense selection of papers and paper products.

F.G. Kettle, Inc.,
127 High Holborn,
London, W.C. 1. England.

Alec Tiranti,
72 Charlotte Street,
London, W.1., England.

ABOUT GLUES

WHITE GLUE: Plastic base made in various formulas by different manufacturers. Popular brands are Elmer's and Sobo. Milky texture turns clear when dry.
Protective coating.
White glue may be thinned with water and used as a protective coating on most papers. Experiment before applying to an important piece of work. For example, tissue paper when treated will change its texture by becoming transparent and stiffer.

PAPER CEMENT: Packaged in a tube or a glass jar with a brush.
Temporary placement.
Brush a coat of paper cement on one surface and put cut-out in place on the background. To reposition, lift one edge and peel gradually.
Permanent Bond.
Coat both surfaces thinly. Allow them to dry. Then press dried surfaces together.
Hints.
Smeared cement can be rubbed off easily when dry. Paper cement is not recommended for any art work which is to last indefinitely, asy more than a few months.

METYLAN (or POLYCELL) PASTE: Another glue to know about. It is similar to wallpaper paste, but does not sour. Mix powder with water according to instructions. Inexpensive and therefore useful for large quantities.